Idlewild Sermons

from

Idlewild Presbyterian Church

Stephen R. Montgomery

To Kathryn,
"You shall love your
neighbor as yourself."
It is easy for Patti and
me to love you — a wonderful
neighbor! With joy and
thanksgiving,
Steve

ppbooks
a good word company

Parson's Porch Books

Idlewild Sermons from Idlewild Presbyterian Church
ISBN: Softcover 978-0692541531
Copyright © 2015 by Stephen R. Montgomery

All scripture quotations are from the *New Revised Standard Version.*

Photo Credits: Matt Matthews, photo on cover of stained glass at Idlewild Presbyterian Church; Fred Toma, photo on back of Dr. Montgomery.

To order additional copies of this book, contact:

Parson's Porch Books
1-423-475-7308
www.parsonsporch.com

Parson's Porch Books is an imprint of Parson's Porch & Company (PP&C) in Cleveland, Tennessee. PP&C is an innovative organization which raises money by publishing books of noted authors, representing all genres. All donations from contributors and profits from publishing are shared with the poor.

Idlewild Sermons

from

Idlewild Presbyterian Church

Table of Contents

Foreword

The collegium of preachers to which Steve Montgomery and I belong now has it plate exceedingly full of expectation, demand, and responsibility. That plate is full because we now live in a culture of commoditization that is bent toward self-destruction and death, in which human persons and creaturely possibility are ruthlessly transposed into marketable goods. The force of that commoditization is immense in the ominous pursuit of security and domination. In the midst of that force, the preacher is expected to speak some good news that is at the same time honest and compelling.

The demands on the preacher are made more difficult because the preacher lives in and must speak to a culture of expansive anxiety. As a result the preacher is aware of how quickly a congregant may take offense, and how promptly a divisive ideology can be provoked. Or more practically, preachers like Steve Montgomery preside over an institutional budget that cannot much tolerate an affront to potential giver.

In the face of such palpable risks, the preacher has only limited means and resources, a book, some water, some bread and wine, and a long memory of witnesses who precede and live alongside us.

This characterization of the preacher's daily work comes to mind as I have read and pondered Steve's sermons. His sermons make several things clear. Steve is fully in touch with the huge dangers and seductions that our society faces, dangers and seductions that are compounded by ready denial and a refusal to think critically. Steve, as a good pastor, has a deep sense of his congregants, of how they may be engaged, so that the truth he speaks is offered in graciousness and gentleness, spoken not to confront or to irritate, but to permit movement (that for most of us is quite slow work) to a new way in the world that is marked by glad gospel obedience.

Most of all, it is apparent that Steve fully understands the means he has at his disposal for his important task of transformative testimony. Given the trivialization and dismissal of "the word" in a culture of rapidly morphing images, he takes word and utterance most seriously, and does so with precision and artistry. As a result his sermons are clear, engaging, honest, and non-coercive. In one of

7

his sermons he ponders the truth that with "one word it all changes."
He is gifted in finding that one word regularly in these sermons, that
one human word that attests the One Word made flesh among us.
Alongside his skill and sensitivity to the word, his utterance is
permeated by compelling sense of the sacramental. He does not
refrain from reminding his congregants of the costly truth of their
baptism or of the sustenance of the Eucharist....not bad for a
Presbyterian!

In the face of these heavy expectations, these sneaky dangers of
dominant culture, and the gifts he mobilizes, Steve is clear that he is
not alone. He travels with good companions who constitute the
communion of saints who also trust the word. Thus his sermons are
well informed by quotes from other master word crafters such as
Anne Lamott and Eugene Peterson and others who twist and turn
us to newness by their utterances. Such citation is not padding but
serves to thicken Steve's own good words in a glad awareness shared
gifts in the community.

As I read these sermons, I imagined how they must have felt, been
heard, and received by Idlewild Presbyterians, a wondrous
congregation where I have on occasion been able to preach. I
imagine that among those congregants, many of them departed
church, as I would have, newly aware of our skewed culture that
waits for bold-counteraction. I imagine they departed, as I would
have, confident that it could, by the mercy of God, be otherwise.
And I imagined that they, like me, felt resummoned to discipleship.
Steve's clarity and imagination fully persuades that the story of Jesus
is "not make-believe. It is rather a genuine alternative. No doubt
these congregants are moved by the artistry of his faithful craft. But
beyond that, they also know that the outcome of such sermons is
not dazzlement but a readiness to go in obedience where they had
not thought to do until this moment of proclamation. In a word,
these sermons are church-making as a lively alternative in a debased
society in which the neighbor or has almost been negated.

I am grateful for these sermons. I am very glad that I belong to the
same preaching collegium alongside Stephen Montgomery.

Walter Brueggemann
Columbia Theological Seminary
August 30, 2015

Preface

Serving as the pastor of the Idlewild Presbyterian Church was not in my game plan. After graduating from the Yale Divinity School, I spent four years serving a small church in the coal fields of Appalachia in Eastern Kentucky; then ten years in a transitional urban residential neighborhood outside of Atlanta, Georgia, followed by six years in another Atlanta area church. I saw myself as anything but a "big steeple" preacher, but rather a servant leader devoting my ministry to those on the margins of society.

But God had other plans, so when I accepted a call to be the pastor of Idlewild, there was a fair amount of awe, wonder, humility and gratitude, but underlying it all was fear. Idlewild has been, for over a century, one of the leading lights in what was the Southern Presbyterian Church, now the Presbyterian Church (USA), known both for its commitment to social justice and urban ministry as well as its awe-inspiring neo-gothic cathedral. I was standing on the shoulders of preachers who articulated powerfully the call to discipleship in the context of their day. How could I possibly measure up?

Though unprepared in many ways, I was grateful for several experiences I had that helped shape my preaching through the years. When Vatican II re-shaped the nature of worship in the Catholic church in the early 1960's, the winds of change blew toward us Protestants, as we began to realize that in many cases we had thrown the baby out with the bathwater. As a result, even "decently and in order" Presbyterians began to experience liturgical renewal. By the time I entered seminary in the 1970's, the Psalter was being used, the Great Prayer of Thanksgiving was incorporated into the Lord's Supper, and most significantly for us preachers, many adopted the lectionary to guide our preaching and worship planning.

Thus, through the years I have given two cheers for the lectionary. It enables a preacher and a congregation to hear the breadth of scripture over a three year cycle. It connects us not only to other traditions, including the Catholic Church, but also the global church. When my wife and I were in Peru for ten weeks as we adopted our first child, it was great comfort to know that the text being used in Lima was the same one being used by our home church in Atlanta. And the lectionary enables preachers, as much as possible, to deal with texts we would just as soon not deal with.

Most of the sermons presented here were preached from the lectionary. Some were from special liturgical days—Baptism of the Lord Sunday, Transfiguration Sunday and the like, but most were from ordinary time. And sometimes the lectionary text went hand in glove with the events of the day—the Sunday after 9/11 or Martin Luther King, Jr. week-end. But sometimes it is helpful, even mandatory, to depart from the three year cycle; hence the "two cheers." During some summers our clergy team has preached series from the Old Testament stories that were indeed lectionary texts, but sometimes we would preach on themes: "Questions from the floor," "Texts I love to hate," and "Biblical and Theological Themes from Children's books." Several are presented here.

In addition to the liturgical renewal, there were new developments in biblical theology, led in part by one of my divinity school professors, Brevard Childs, who began to re-think the church's interpretation of the biblical canon. Though his influence is presently declining in the academic guild, his contributions were significant.

But for me the greatest influence was a small book that came out the year I graduated by Walter Brueggemann, *The Prophetic Imagination.* At a time when I was filled with enough biblical knowledge to answer any questions, but was wondering if it really was important to know what happened to the Jebusites and what that had to do with the war in El Salvador or the poverty here in our own country. Rejecting the liberal tendency which might care about the politics of justice and compassion but largely uninterested in the freedom of God; but also rejecting more conservative tendencies to care intensely about God, but uncritically, so that the God of well-being and good order is not understood to be precisely the source of social oppression, the book transformed my approach to scriptures.

Brueggemann called for an alternative reality, beginning with Moses and extending through the prophets, culminating in Jesus of Nazareth. Prophetic ministry consists of offering an alternative perception of reality and in letting people see their own history in the light of God's freedom and God's will for justice.

This means that true prophetic preaching is witness, affirmation, and proclamation that God is, that God reigns, and that God does not abandon or forget. Thus, there is always a movement toward hope, which is not simply an add-on at the end of a sermon. Rather, hope is intrinsic to the prophetic message. The prophetic themes of destruction and restoration yield to the central Christian themes of crucifixion and resurrection. For God is always doing a new thing, creating a way where there is no way, and bringing life out of death, light out of very real darkness.

These sermons are admittedly feeble attempts to encourage us (for one of the listeners to the sermon is the preacher!) to trust that God reigns, and to imagine a world as God intends it and as God works to bring it around. I hope that they acknowledge what is often denied: loss, grief, destruction; but that defeat, disillusionment, and even death, are not dead ends but signs of an impending resurrection if we have the faith to live fully in that contradiction and live in hope.

Through the past 35 years there have been countless others I have carried with me into the pulpit, teachers like Fred Craddock (whose formative book *As One Without Authority* came out my first year of seminary) and Tom Long; as well as fellow preachers, mentors and friends like John Buchanan, Jon Walton, Barbara Brown Taylor, Barbara Lundblad, and Ted Wardlaw; not to mention my friend and rabbi Micah Greenstein at Temple Israel here in Memphis, who has made me a better Christian (and hopefully preacher) by teaching me about the faith of Jesus, and reminding me of the hope and imagination embedded in the prophets.

I am grateful to them all, but am especially grateful to the congregation of Idlewild Presbyterian Church. To preach to a congregation that honors the freedom of the pulpit and expects a faithful reading of the bible in one hand and scripture in the other (as Karl Barth suggested); to be on the receiving end of open hearts and minds; to be invited into their lives and expose my own vulnerabilities, doubts, and possibly even heresies, my heart could not be more full of gratitude. Grace has abounded.

I have learned far more about preaching…and ministry in general…. from the associates I have served with at Idlewild: Andrew and Kate Foster Connors, Margaret Burnett, Gayle Walker, Casey Thompson, Anne H.K. Apple, and Rebekah Abel Lamar. To be able to walk through the scriptures each Tuesday with them as we prepared the worship service, and then to reflect with them the week following is a gift any preacher would be envious of.

It goes without saying that no collection of sermons could be proofread, assembled, and edited without saints like Carol Good, Ginny Moore, and Jenni Brooks. As a borderline Luddite who still is learning the basics of computer 101, I offer my thanks.

Most of all, I am grateful for my wife Patti, and our two children Aaron and Sumita. Patti, a born and bred Yankee Catholic, met this born and bred Southern Presbyterian, and agreed to marry me. From the Ivy League walls of divinity school, to the hollers of Appalachia, to the carillon bells of a gothic tower, she has been my biggest support and confidant, asking basic, honest questions about the faith that all preachers need to hear and address. She, Aaron, and Sumita have constantly reminded me what is truly important in life, and have grounded me in my full humanity by accepting and loving me for who I am, foibles and all. They have made me a better person, and I hope a better pastor and preacher. It is to them that I dedicate this book.

A Dividing Wall
July 23, 2006

Ephesians 2:11–22

11 So then, remember that at one time you Gentiles by birth, called "the uncircumcision" by those who are called "the circumcision"—a physical circumcision made in the flesh by human hands— 12 remember that you were at that time without Christ, being aliens from the commonwealth of Israel, and strangers to the covenants of promise, having no hope and without God in the world. 13 But now in Christ Jesus you who once were far off have been brought near by the blood of Christ.

14 For he is our peace; in his flesh he has made both groups into one and has broken down the dividing wall, that is, the hostility between us. 15 He has abolished the law with its commandments and ordinances, that he might create in himself one new humanity in place of the two, thus making peace, 16 and might reconcile both groups to God in one body through the cross, thus putting to death that hostility through it. 17 So he came and proclaimed peace to you who were far off and peace to those who were near; 18 for through him both of us have access in one Spirit to the Father. 19 So then you are no longer strangers and aliens, but you are citizens with the saints and also members of the household of God, 20 built upon the foundation of the apostles and prophets, with Christ Jesus himself as the cornerstone. 21 In him the whole structure is joined together and grows into a holy temple in the Lord; 22 in whom you also are built together spiritually into a dwelling place for God.

Prayer: Dear God, all we have to do is open the morning newspaper to realize that there are dividing walls of hostility all around this world you created, even walls in our own hearts. So we come to you seeking your peace, because sometimes that's all we have. Help us to hold tightly to your vision of a world at peace, beginning with our own lives. Startle us with your love for the whole world. Amen.

A FEW YEARS BEFORE THE END OF THE cold war, when the Berlin Wall was still up, separating east from west, First world from Second world, communism from capitalism, Germany from Germany, Dr. Seuss wrote one of his final books which is just as relevant today as it was then. And just as relevant in Paul's day as today. It was called *The Butter Battle Book*. Here's how it starts:

> On the last day of summer, ten hours before fall…

> …my grandfather took me out to the Wall. For a while he stood silent.

> Then finally he said, with a very sad shake of his very old head,
> "As you know...on this side of the Wall we are Yooks.

> On the far side of this Wall Live the Zooks."
> Then my grandfather said, "It's high time that you knew

> Of the terribly horrible thing that Zooks do. In every Zook house and in every Zook town Every Zook eats his bread

14

With the butter side down!! But we Yooks, as you
know, when we breakfast or sup,

Spread our bread," Grandpa said, "With the butter
side up.
That's the right, honest way!" Grandpa gritted his
teeth.
"So you can't trust a Zook who spreads bread
underneath! Every Zook must be watched." 1

From there on Grandpa gives his grandson a lesson in how hostilities
escalated over the years between the Yooks and the Zooks. They
developed bigger and better and more powerful weapons as the wall
grew higher and higher. There was the Triple Sling Jigger, the Kick-
a-Poo-Kid, and the biggest, baddest of all weapons, the Bitsy Big-
Boy Boomeroo, a tiny bomb that could destroy the whole world. At
the very end of the book there is a Zook and a Yook standing on
top of the wall, each holding a Bitsy Big-Boy Boomeroo, wondering
who will be the first to drop the bomb and destroy each of them.

I wonder what it is about us humans that so thrives on hostility.
What is it about us that loves a wall? Some ethnologists and social
scientists like Konrad Lorenz and Desmond Morris say that hostility
and aggression are basic human instincts that we shall never rid of.
Others, like Ashley Montagu tell us that such behavior is learned,
and we can become educated not to hate.

Scripture, in a sense, says that there is truth in both. Hostility is not
part of our essential nature, it is part of our fallen nature. If we
eliminated it, we would not become less than human; we would
become as fully human as God intends. And yet all antagonisms that

alienate us from one another are symptomatic of our alienation from God. Or, to use a word that has fallen into disuse, sin.

The walls are always there, and we seem to love them. Just as one wall goes down (the Berlin Wall), another wall goes up. (Right now it looks like there will be a wall between the U.S. and Mexico.) Or just as we mend one broken relationship, say, with a friend, there is another one that breaks. I am continually amazed at how creative we can be at devising walls to separate us from one another.

One of my jobs in college was chauffeuring speakers and dignitaries from the Cleveland airport to Wooster, which was about 60 miles away. The very first time I did that I had to pick up a man whom I had never heard of. He wasn't a household name at that point, but I had a sign with his name on it there at the airport and he found me, and I had a fascinating ride back to Wooster. He was full of exuberance because he was telling me about a book he was finishing up, and he had just come back from Africa where he had traced his ancestral roots. His name was Alex Haley.

But what I remembered most was his recollection of a trip to Ireland he took to do some research. "Yes," he told me when I looked somewhat bemused, "I'm part Irish. The Klan would have fits if they knew that." As he was going over there he wondered how he would be treated because of the color of his skin, and to his great delight, the family that hosted him received him warmly. They fixed a veritable banquet, laughed and told stories. He couldn't believe it. But around mid-evening he noticed that the atmosphere changed. His hosts cooled immediately. It turns out that he mentioned that he was Protestant. And they escorted him out of that part of the city to a wall, which he crossed over to stay in another part of the city. If we didn't have enemies, we'd have to invent them. We so love our walls.

The Gentiles in the early church knew something about barriers and walls. Did you notice how many ways Paul emphasized that? They were the ones who were "far off," the "uncircumcised," those "alienated from the commonwealth of Israel," "strangers to the covenants of promise," "having no hope and without God in the world."

Paul might be the last person in the world one would think who might be sensitive to the Gentiles' plight. After all, he began as a Pharisee, proud of his exclusive ethnic and religious identity. He knew something about walls, all right, because he had spent his life constructing walls that separated him from the unclean Gentiles.

Imagine the energy it took to maintain that barrier. You see, that barrier was symbolized by an actually dividing wall in the Temple in Jerusalem. The Temple was divided into four courts—the center court was the "Court of the Priests," who were considered the most holy of all and who made sure all the laws were kept that ensured purity on their part; then surrounding that was the "Court of the Israelites," then the "Court of the Women." As one got further and further away one became less pure, less holy. And then there was a dividing wall. It separated the Court of the Women from the Court of the Gentiles. And on top of that stone wall dividing the two courts was an inscription which forbade any foreigner to go in under the pain of death.

Yes, the Gentiles knew something about barriers, and so did Paul. But from the day that Paul was knocked off his horse on the road to Damascus and blinded and turned around by God, he began a

17

theological journey from narrow exclusivism to a broad, open, grace filled theology of the cross which concluded that God sent Jesus, not just to save a few fortunate ones who happened to be lucky enough to hear the news and believe it, but to heal and restore and redeem the whole creation! God's purpose in Jesus Christ is as big as the world itself.

And so near the end of his life, Paul was writing things like:

"In Christ Jesus you who once were far off have been brought near by the blood of Christ…He is our peace…he has broken down the dividing wall, that is, the hostility between us."

In his life, Christ never stopped crossing over those barriers of his day—barriers between Jew and Gentile, Jew and Samaritan, between male and female, Pharisee and Sadducee, Scribe and Zealot, rich and poor, adult and child, righteous and sinner. He crossed over every barrier he ever encountered, and it led to his death, and in his death on the cross, he tore down the barrier between life and death, and thus every barrier that would separate us from one another.

I am convinced that there is no more important calling for Christians today than to come out from behind those walls and live in the marvelous freedom of God's unconditional love, so that we no longer need to be strangers and aliens, but may become fellow citizens in the household of God, joined together in Christ.

It can begin with the walls in our very hearts, where hostility begins, with those that we love the most, but those who for some reason we push away even as we try to draw close. Anne Lamott tells the story of being on the beach one day with her mother around the Fourth of July. The story is prompted by a photograph taken by a friend, which shows Lamott and her mother holding hands that day. She remembers that she was annoyed with her mother, in spite of the warmth and affection that one might assume from the picture. It is a story about an internal war and reconciliation. She writes:

"I was annoyed that day because my mother acts so much older than she is. She is only 73, but she staggers along the sand like a toddler. I was annoyed because she had asked me once again with anxious hope if I had met anyone nice. I was annoyed because dark pink lipstick was smeared on her front teeth…I was annoyed because we were waiting for my younger brother and my son to meet us at the beach for a Fourth of July party at a friend's house and each time my brother's name was mentioned, my mother acted like a Frank Sinatra fan. Also, she is so needy: she needs me to pull her to her feet when she's been sitting down, needs to grip my hand tightly when she walks, as though we were on a tightrope instead of a beach, she needs me to retrieve her lipstick from inside our friend's house…..Also, I secretly believed she could do better if she tried, that —perhaps this sounds paranoid—she acts this way to torture and control me. In my worst moments, I imagine her at home just before I pick her up, wearing a telephone headset and berating some commodities trader. Then when she hears me knock, she dashes to her bedroom, stashes the headset, pulls on her Ruth Buzzi cardigan, applies lipstick to her teeth, and totters to the front door to let me in.

"On the beach," she continues, "I hold her hand and feel that my heart could break with love for her. Ten minutes later I find myself growling at her when she's out of earshot, when she's sitting on the sand waiting for me to return with her lipstick."

In the end Anne sees what is going on. "Sometimes, holding her soft warm hand, I want to take it and hurl it to the sand beneath the wheels of the oncoming lifeguard's jeep. But oh, God, the trust with which she keeps holding it out for me to take. Without someone to steady her, she cannot find her balance. And I guess when you take away the resentment and disappointment, it's that simple. It is what we do in families: we help, because we were helped." 2

Don't we all live with that tension inside us of needing to draw close and to push away those whom we love, and those whom we barely love? Paul tells us that God is in the business of creating a stunning new humanity.

Can you believe that when you read the newspaper or see the violence erupting in Lebanon while we enjoy (?) our dinner? How does all of this happen? Talk to an Israeli and they speak the truth: Can you imagine what it must be like to live in a small country surrounded by countries and groups that want your annihilation? Talk to a Lebanese and they speak the truth: Can you imagine what it must be like to hear the missiles coming your way that might be headed toward your very children? Can you believe Paul?

Michael Lindvall, pastor of the Brick Presbyterian Church in New York City, tells in a book he wrote about a friend of his, Fuad Bahnan, an Arab Christian pastor in Beirut after the last Israeli-Arab world. In 1983, Israeli armies drove into Lebanon—and members of the church began to buy all the canned food they could to survive a rumored Israeli siege. That's what happened. West Beirut was totally cut-off. And so the Session of the church met to decide how to distribute the food they had purchased. Two proposals were put on the table. The first was to distribute food to the church members, then other Christians; and last, if any was left, to Muslim neighbors. The other proposal was different. First food would be given to Muslim neighbors, then to other Christians, and finally, if there was any left over, to church members.

Idlewild Sermons

The meeting lasted six hours. "It ended when an older, quiet, much respected elder, a woman, stood up and said, "If we do not demonstrate the love of Christ in this place, who will?" And so the second motion passed." 3

That...is....our.... calling! To claim what Christ did for us on the cross. To say to those hostilities in our hearts and in our lives that we have used to build walls between each other: "You're dead. You're finished. Christ has done you in! I am free to quit spending my energies into hate and hostility and building walls, and now I am free... free to love. Because that's the final word."

He is our peace, and has broken down the dividing wall. Thanks be to God!

Amen.

[1] Dr. Seuss, The Butter Battle Book, Random House, 1984.
[2] Anne Lamott, Traveling Mercies, New York: Pantheon, 1999, p. 210-211.
[3] Michael Lindvall, The Christian Life: A Geography of God, Louisville: Geneva Press, 2001, p. 126.

21

Amber Waves of Grain

July 4, 2010
(Independence Day)

Deuteronomy 8

1 This entire commandment that I command you today you must diligently observe, so that you may live and increase, and go in and occupy the land that the Lord promised on oath to your ancestors. 2 Remember the long way that the Lord your God has led you these forty years in the wilderness, in order to humble you, testing you to know what was in your heart, whether or not you would keep his commandments. 3 He humbled you by letting you hunger, then by feeding you with manna, with which neither you nor your ancestors were acquainted, in order to make you understand that one does not live by bread alone, but by every word that comes from the mouth of the Lord. 4 The clothes on your back did not wear out and your feet did not swell these forty years. 5 Know then in your heart that as a parent disciplines a child so the Lord your God disciplines you. 6 Therefore keep the commandments of the Lord your God, by walking in his ways and by fearing him. 7 For the Lord your God is bringing you into a good land, a land with flowing streams, with springs and underground waters welling up in valleys and hills, 8 a land of wheat and barley, of vines and fig trees and pomegranates, a land of olive trees and honey, 9 a land where you may eat bread without scarcity, where you will lack nothing, a land whose stones are iron and from whose hills you may mine copper. 10 You shall eat your fill and bless the Lord your God for the good land that he has given you. 11 Take care that you do not forget the Lord your God, by failing to keep his commandments, his ordinances, and his statutes, which I am commanding you today. 12 When you have eaten your fill and have built fine houses and live in them, 13 and when your herds and flocks have multiplied, and your silver and gold is multiplied, and all that you have is multiplied, 14 then do not exalt yourself, forgetting the Lord your God, who brought you out of the land of Egypt, out of the house of slavery, 15 who led you through the great and terrible wilderness, an arid wasteland with poisonous snakes and scorpions. He made water flow for you from flint rock, 16 and fed you in the wilderness with manna that your ancestors did not know, to humble you and to test you, and in the end to do you good. 17 Do not say to yourself, "My power and the might of my own hand have gotten me this wealth." 18 But remember the Lord your God, for it is he who gives you power to get wealth, so that he may confirm his covenant that he swore to your ancestors, as he is doing today. 19 If you do forget the Lord your God and follow other gods to serve and worship them, I solemnly warn you today that you shall surely perish. 20 Like the nations that the Lord is destroying before you, so shall you perish, because you would not obey the voice of the Lord your God.

Prayer: We thank you, O God, for the blessings of liberty, for the simple but beautiful privilege of reading a newspaper this morning which has not been censored, for the privilege of deciding to invest this morning in worship, free from control or encouragement, for the freedom to believe in your or not to believe in you. Author of liberty, startle us with your love which frees us from everything that would oppress or demean or hold us back, in Jesus Christ our Lord. Amen.

I T WAS A MOMENTOUS DAY! A NEW LAND WAS about to be settled, a new nation about to be established. Previously the people had been NO people, construction slaves on the Nile River, nomad wanderers in the Sinai Desert. People with no voice and no clout, people pushed about by the overwhelming power of others. But now all of this was to change. These people were about to occupy a territory which they had been promised, and to establish a nation which would be among the great ones of the earth. All present waited in anxious anticipation.

It was clear that the land they were about to receive was a gift, a gift of the ancient God who had come to them in their oppression. This God had led them out of their bondage with a mighty hand and an outstretched arm. This God had led them with signs and wonders through the desert wilderness. This God had brought them to the place where they were now encamped, in the Plains of Moab, just east of the Jordan River, from which, for the first time, they gazed upon the rich and fertile land which was to become theirs.

As they looked, they were overwhelmed. Not at all the parched desert wasteland which had been their home for the past 40 years, this was a land of grandeur: a land of brooks and water, of fountains and springs, flowing forth in valleys and hills, a land of wheat and barley, of vines and fig trees and pomegranates, a land of spacious skies and amber waves of grain, of purple mountain majesties above the fruited plain, a land whose stones were iron and whose hills were copper, a land where God had spread God's grace liberally from sea to shining sea. This was to become their land, a gift from God, their inheritance through many generations.

On the eve of their entry, their leader, Moses, gathered them together to make a speech concerning what they were about to do. We can see the whole assembly seated on a mountainside with Moses, standing on a high place, setting forth his words. It was a key moment in the life of the people, a major turning point between past and future. Moses addressed this turning point, and spoke directly to what was to be.

First, he raised a primary question: Why has God chosen you? Why did God not choose the Moabites or the Ammonites or the

Philistines? Why you? Was it because you were more deserving than they, more virtuous, of a higher moral fiber? To answer this question, Moses reviewed the story of Israel's life so far: You were an unknown people in the land of Egypt, nothing among the nations. After God heard your cries and delivered you at the Red Sea, you became a stubborn and stiff-necked people, murmuring because you were thirsty, complaining because you were hungry, and making for yourselves golden calves because you did not believe that God could care for you. You fought and bickered and broke the commandments. You turned aside and worshipped other gods. Did God choose you because you were deserving? God chose you because God chose you—for no other reason. An act of pure grace. It was God's doing and not yours that you are here today.

Moses then turned to consider the life they would life in the land they were about to occupy. After you settle I the land, he said, after you drink it was water and eat from its amber waves of grain, after you build for yourselves goodly houses and alabaster cities, after you come to enjoy the best fruits of this rich place, then, at that moment, you will face the greatest question of your existence, the fundamental issue of your entire life: What effect will this prosperity have on you?

What kind of people will this gift of God make you? Will your head be puffed up? Will you say in your heart, "Behold, my power and the might of my hands have gotten me this wealth?" Will you come to think that it is your own initiative and worth that have brought you where you are? Or will you remember how the Lord your God brought you out of the land of oppression, and led you through the great and terrible wilderness with its fiery serpents and scorpions and thirsty ground, and brought you this place?

What effect will this prosperity have on you? Will it make you blind shield your eyes against those who have not been given this same abundance, harden your heart against them? Will you lie down on beds of ivory, and stretch yourselves on plush couches, eat the best lambs from the flock and filet mignon from the midst of the stall, sing idle songs to the sound of the harp and enjoy the best in classical performance, will you drink wine in bowls and bathe yourselves in the finest oils, and take no notice of the destitute who are all around you?

Or will you reach forth your hand in mercy to the meek and lowly, to the downtrodden and the oppressed, to provide for them as your God provided for you?

What effect will this prosperity have on you? Will it make you a vineyard of sour grapes? When the Lord comes to measure you for justice and test you for righteousness, will he find instead bloodshed and a cry of anguish? Will oppression roll down like waters and exploitation like an ever-flowing stream? Will you grind the heads of the powerless into the dust of the earth, and turn aside the way of the afflicted? Will court decisions be sold in the marketplace and favorable treatment auctioned to the highest bidder?

Or will justice be your guide and righteousness be your light? Will you decide with equity between the strong and the powerless? Will your words convey truth and your pronouncements reality? Will the vineyard produce sweet grapes which its builder intended?

What effect will this prosperity have on you? Will you measure your worth by economic accomplishment, your status by the size of your estate? Will you come to believe that because you are prosperous, you are superior?

Or will you count yourself fortunate that you were born in an historical moment when the toil of your hands produced grain and barley rather than thorns and thistles, when the talents of your minds led to success rather than to frustration?

In other words, the key question as you move into this land is: will the prosperity that God is giving you make you haughty or make you thankful? Will it cause you to crawl off into your own perfected world of enriched splendor, surrounded by an ever-increasing abundance of lavish things, sealed off from the hard realities of the rest of humanity, or will it cause you to live a fundamentally grateful life, using your gifts so that others also shall receive blessing? Will it make you self-centered or self-giving? This is the speech that Moses spoke to Israel on the eve of their entry into the Promised Land.

It is significant that 600 years later, in the reign of King Josiah, after Israel had had a long and varied history, some prophets found a copy of this speech in the Jerusalem archives and declared it to the nation a second time as God's work spoken through Moses. The prophets perceived that even a country that is six centuries old still stands on the threshold of what it shall become, and still faces this fundamental issue of its life.

Today we celebrate the 234th anniversary of the United States of America. We shall sing of spacious skies and amber waves of grain. We shall pray for God's continued blessing from the mountains, to the prairies, to the oceans white with foam. We shall give thanks for this land of freedom and prosperity which are gifts from God.

And as we do so, the fundamental question that God poses to us remains the same. The question has not changed in 3,200 years: What kind of people, what kind of nation, will the prosperity of this land make you?

Will we say in our hearts, "My power and the might of my hand have gotten me this wealth?" And will our basic approach to life be protectiveness and greed?

Or will we say, "These amber waves of grain are God's gift to me to be used as a blessing for many?"

This is the issue as we, the United States of America, on this momentous day, encamp in the Plains of Moab, on the threshold of what we shall become.

And there is no better starting place to answer that question than at the table, where we are reminded to whom our allegiance ultimately belongs, and who is the giver of all good gifts.

Thanks be to God.

Come on in, the Water's Fine!

January 12, 2014
(Baptism of Our Lord Sunday)

Matthew 3:13-17

13The reason I speak to them in parables is that 'seeing they do not perceive, and hearing they do not listen, nor do they understand.' 14With them indeed is fulfilled the prophecy of Isaiah that says: 'You will indeed listen, but never understand, and you will indeed look, but never perceive. 15For this people's heart has grown dull, and their ears are hard of hearing, and they have shut their eyes; so that they might not look with their eyes, and listen with their ears, and understand with their heart and turn— and I would heal them.' 16But blessed are your eyes, for they see, and your ears, for they hear. 17Truly I tell you, many prophets and righteous people longed to see what you see, but did not see it, and to hear what you hear, but did not hear it.

Prayer: Still-speaking God, as these words from Scripture are read, may it be to us as if the heavens are opening, and we see your Spirit descending on us, like a dove, revealing your love for us as your daughters and sons. Amen.

L IVING BY THE MISSISSIPPI RIVER, IT DOESN'T take long to understand the power of a river. A river will eventually transform anything it flows over, or anyone who walks through it or lives by it. It can bring death, when it floods and drowns; or life, in the fertility it gives at its banks.

There is a river that runs through scripture. It is the Jordan. Found at the center of the biblical landscape, it serves as a barrier and a border, as life-bringer and death-dealer. The Israelites, after wandering in the wilderness for 40 years following their liberation from Egypt, cross the Jordan, passing into the Promised Land.

The prophets later speak of God's Spirit one day crossing back over the Jordan and bringing good news to those beyond its boundaries. Isaiah writes: "In the latter time God will make glorious…the land beyond the Jordan, Galilee of the nations."

Life in Palestine then, and to a large extent now, is defined by which side of the river you live on.

For African slaves in 19th century America, the Ohio River was known as the River Jordan, because it was the crossing over point from slavery in the south to freedom in the north. Those brave men and women and children often saw themselves as latter-day Israelites, entering the Promised Land by passing through the river. God works in the water.

In the time of Jesus, the one called John spent a lot of time at the river. That's why they called him the Baptizer. John knew the power of the water to clean or to drown, to quench thirst and to give new life. For all who went down and came up out of it, it was the sign that a new day had come, that the past was washed away. A sign of forgiveness of their sin. A sign of their welcome into a new life, made whole by the grace of God, down by the river.

One of my favorite movie scenes is from that now-classic movie "O Brother, Where Art Thou," which happens at the river. The story is set in the Deep South during the Depression. Three white convicts named Pete, Delmar, and Ulysses escape from their chain gang. The film is the account of their wandering in the wilderness, hoping to reach a sort of Promised Land. The sheriff, who is the devil with a badge on, is in hot pursuit.

At one point in their odyssey they are hiding in the woods, eating a meal of roasted gopher, when all of a sudden they hear around them the sound of angelic singing. Delmar, who is not the brightest fellow, stops eating and listens, "It appears to be some sort of congregation," he says.

He's right, and the congregation is headed for the river. Drawn by their singing, their white robes through the trees, the look of joy on their faces, the three convicts follow. Delmar is particularly mesmerized by the scene at the river. The three escapees stand there, gaping as men and women come forward to be dipped under the muddy current by the minister.

Delmar is desperate for what they are receiving. He is transfixed by what he sees. Unable to hold back, he plunges in, splashing over to the baptizer who takes him, utters the words of baptism, and thrusts him under the water. A moment later he comes up, grinning at the new-ness of everything. Pete, who has been taking it all in at the river bank, says, "Well I'll be. Delmar's been saved."

Delmar leaps with joy in the water. "Well, that's it, boys," he cries. "I've been redeemed! The preacher done washed away all my sins and transgressions. I'm on the straight and narrow from here on out, and heaven everlastin' is my reward!"

Delmar is beside himself with relief. "The preacher says all my sins is washed away, includin' that Piggly Wiggly I knocked over in Yazoo."

A skeptical Ulysses says, "I thought you said you was innocent of those charges."

Delmar replies, "Well, I was lyin', and the preacher says that that sin's been washed away, too. Neither God nor man's got nothing on me now." And then throwing his arms up, he shouts, "Come on in, boys, the water's fine!"

That, my friends, is one of the great theological lines in the history of cinema: Come on in, the water's fine. What a magnificent portrayal in that scene of the power of the Holy Spirit to work through the waters of baptism to generate human life.

Now, I don't know if John yelled to Jesus, "Come on in, Jesus, the water's fine! The Spirit is ready for you!" But John did know that the Holy Spirit working in that waster held the secret to new life, the cleansing of our past, the forgiveness of sins, a call to repentance, to turn our lives around, and a permanent welcome into the community of the redeemed.

You know, for the early church, the baptism of Jesus was a scandal. How could they explain it? Why would Jesus have to get baptized? Was he there to wash away his sins? To accept the forgiveness of God? I think even Jesus wanted to belong, to be a part of the community of those who, like Delmar, can turn to the rest of us on the riverbank and say "Come on in! The water's fine." Even Jesus needed to hear what all of us need to hear: "You are my beloved child". Isn't that something that you have yearned for in those days that you feel you've really blown it? In those nights when you are alone and wonder if it's all worth it? Those times you have been bullied by classmates, bosses, and society? When for whatever reason you have been made to feel that you are unworthy?

32

I remember when I was in seminary, with loans up to my neck both from college and divinity school. Working two jobs, skimping on everything I could. Late at night I turned on the little black and white TV we had and there was a commercial for a flight from New York City to Miami. Only $99. The announcer said "Anyone can afford it!" I'm sorry, but there was no way I could afford it. It might have been subtle, but the message I got was that I was nobody.

Jesus needed to be a part of the community. He needed to hear who he was from God: My Son, the beloved one.

I once heard Walter Brueggemann talk about the power of various scripts to define us. The dominant script in our culture, as he described it, is that we are isolated autonomous beings, each one of us; that we are endowed with limitless possibility, that progress is ours that we can live independently of one another. The dominant script is that we are capable of providing all that we need or want all by ourselves that things matter over people, and more things matter more. It is that dominant script that determines who we are.

Baptism, he said, completely changes "the script" of our lives and of our world. Baptism, beginning with the baptism of Jesus, inaugurates an utterly different worldview. Love is introduced in a new way, a love more powerful than our desire to go it alone, more powerful than our tendency to disengage from the plight of the poor or those on the margins.

Isaiah saw it coming. Do you remember all those Advent texts? There is the script of the world, saying this is the way it is and always will be. But there is now a counter-movement, texts that refuse to give in to the way things are and have been for many years. It is the script that says life is more than just a series of acquisitions, then you die; that life demands more from us than striving for our self-sufficient autonomy and endless consumption. Baptism gets it all rolling.

It is a power that comes from beyond. The heavens open when John dips Jesus; a voice calls out, "This is my Son, the Beloved, with whom I am well pleased." Every time we baptize, the same voice speaks. It is not part of the official baptismal service, but maybe we should add it, as we pour the water over the baby's head: "This is my child, the beloved, with whom I am well pleased."

It is the debut of love, deep, covenantal love, a love deeper than anything we had ever known. It is full of grace and it can know you off your feet like the current in the river.

Most of the times when we have baptisms, there is a little child present, and the parents, children, and the congregation all take vows. Hopefully, years later, that child will come to know something personally about the power and love of God to transform lives. But I remember one particular baptism I had in another church. A young woman would come from time to time to our church because she was a violinist, and we would pay her to play. One Sunday I saw her in church on a Sunday in which she wasn't playing. She kept on coming back, and told me that she wanted what it was that she saw in the congregation.

So, like Delmar, one day she came to the river. Oh, this river was a baptismal font in the front of the church. And she didn't get dunked. I sprinkled her three times. But she was completely overwhelmed by the power of her baptism into the community of the redeemed, so stunned by the experience that she could not go to work for several days afterward. She simply told her employer that she needed time to recover from the baptism. Her life looked entirely different. You see, her script had changed.

34

It was for her, as it was for Delmar, and for Jesus, and for each of us, the debut of a love stronger than any she had ever known in her life. That love has the power to transform, the power to withstand whatever the world throws at us in the end, even death itself.

I like the way Presbyterian pastor Eugene Peterson paraphrased what God said as Jesus came up out of the water: "This is my Son, chosen and marked by my love, delight of my life." I am glad that Jesus heard that affirmation early on because there is much about life that is anything but delightful. The scripts are powerful.

Trevor learned that lesson at an early age. Unlike Delmar, Trevor is a real life boy living in a God-forsaken, drug-infested, violent-riddled part of the Bronx. Heidi Neumark, a young Lutheran pastor was assigned to serve a church which had seen its better days, which was somewhat of an understatement. She wrote, "On Sunday mornings, Trevor got himself and his younger brother and sister up and dressed for church while his mother slept off the highs and lows of the night before. On the day of Trevor's own baptism his mother promised to come, and I believe that she meant it at the time she said it. Through the service, Trevor kept one eye on the door. I did too, but his mom never made it. I asked Trevor if he wanted to wait for another Sunday, but he wanted to go ahead. Trevor bowed his head over the baptismal font and listened to the voice of love that washed over his broken heart. "You are my beloved son with whom I am absolutely delighted. Those were words spoken at Jesus' baptism. We read them for Trevor."

And we read them for every child, youth, and adult who comes to the baptized waters to be reminded: You are my beloved, with whom I am absolutely delighted. Those words follow us all the days of our life, not like some magical shield, but as a new script that gives us the confidence to walk boldly into God's future, confident that our journey of faith will never take us outside the realm of God's delightful grace.

So, come on in. The water's fine, and the love, powerful---powerful enough to wash us and redeem us, and welcome us, and even change us.

Thanks be to God.

Dear Abby…

September 18, 2005

(In Response to Hurricane Katrina)

Exodus 16:2-15

2 The whole congregation of the Israelites complained against Moses and Aaron in the wilderness. 3 The Israelites said to them, "If only we had died by the hand of the Lord in the land of Egypt, when we sat by the fleshpots and ate our fill of bread; for you have brought us out into this wilderness to kill this whole assembly with hunger." 4 Then the Lord said to Moses, "I am going to rain bread from heaven for you, and each day the people shall go out and gather enough for that day. In that way I will test them, whether they will follow my instruction or not. 5 On the sixth day, when they prepare what they bring in, it will be twice as much as they gather on other days." 6 So Moses and Aaron said to all the Israelites, "In the evening you shall know that it was the Lord who brought you out of the land of Egypt, 7 and in the morning you shall see the glory of the Lord, because he has heard your complaining against the Lord. For what are we, that you complain against us?" 8 And Moses said, "When the Lord gives you meat to eat in the evening and your fill of bread in the morning, because the Lord has heard the complaining that you utter against him—what are we? Your complaining is not against us but against the Lord." 9 Then Moses said to Aaron, "Say to the whole congregation of the Israelites, 'Draw near to the Lord, for he has heard your complaining.' "10 And as Aaron spoke to the whole congregation of the Israelites, they looked toward the wilderness, and the glory of the Lord appeared in the cloud. 11 The Lord spoke to Moses and said, 12 "I have heard the complaining of the Israelites; say to them, "At twilight you shall eat meat, and in the morning you shall have your fill of bread; then you shall know that I am the Lord your God.' "

13 In the evening quails came up and covered the camp; and in the morning there was a layer of dew around the camp. 14 When the layer of dew lifted, there on the surface of the wilderness was a fine flaky substance, as fine as frost on the ground. 15 When the Israelites saw it, they said to one another, "What is it?" For they did not know what it was. Moses said to them, "It is the bread that the Lord has given you to eat.

Prayer: As we gather here again this morning, God, we come in the face of mystery. Grant us not answers, but your presence as we listen together for the word you have for us. Help us to know again the power of your redeeming love in Jesus Christ our Lord. Amen.

DEAR DR. STEVE," THE EMAIL BEGAN, "I'M glad you are back. I have a question. Why does God make hurricanes and things like that and take peoples' lives and homes and possessions? Love, Abby."

That was a note written to me last week by one of our better theologians, a nine year old girl named Abby. I can tell you her name because I have permission to do so. I say that she is one of our better theologians because she is not afraid to ask the really hard questions and she is honest about her search. And since it was such a good question, I wanted to share it with you because it's my guess that Abby was not the only one asking that question over the past two weeks. "Why does God make hurricanes and things like that and take people's lives and homes and possessions?"

So here is my response to Abby. If any of you want to listen in, please feel free.

"Dear Abby,

I can't begin to thank you enough for the note you sent me with the question about why God makes hurricanes and things like that and causes bad things to happen. Believe me, it's a question that I ask a lot. I see all kinds of needless suffering, and even I ask "Why?" "Where are you, God?" "How can a loving God do this?"

So I'm just going to share with you how I have come to deal with questions like that. It doesn't mean that it's the only way; it might not even be the right way, to answer those questions, but it's the best that I have come up with so far. And if you have any other suggestions or responses, let me know. Perhaps we can help each other.

The first thing I need to say is that I really don't know the answer. Oh, I know preachers are supposed to have all the answers, and if you asked some other preachers, they might be very sure of their answers. Some will say that God sends hurricanes and floods to punish people. I have actually heard some people say that God didn't like what was going on in New Orleans, so God showed 'em! They got what they deserved!

But Abby, I don't believe that for a minute. God does not want any of God's children to suffer. God doesn't zap us like that if we step out of line.

Some will say that God wants to teach us a lesson, so God sends tragedies down to us so that we might learn something. Well, I'm the first to admit that we can learn some things...a lot of things...about events like this, but once again, I can't believe that God would cause the deaths of hundreds, or leave thousands homeless in order to teach us a lesson.

39

Some would say, like Thomas Jefferson did, that God created the world, wound it up like a clock, and then walked away, allowing it to run on its own without being further involved. That's not for me either. I believe that God is very much involved in our world today, and loves us too much to walk away from us.

There are a lot of different explanations, and some people seem to have all the answers and seem to know it all. I'm not one of those, Abby. As a matter of fact, there was a man who lived five centuries ago named Nicholas of Cusa who said that one of God's greatest gifts to us is "to know that we do not know." Nicholas said that the most ignorant people in the world are those who think they know. If you think you know everything, you can't learn anything new! So they're really in the dark about things that matter.

Abby, I like what someone once said: "There is one thing worse than giving no answer, and that is to give an answer." This month I will have been ordained 25 years as a minister, and I'm going to have to be honest and say I can't explain disasters and tragedies like Katrina.

But I do have something. And so do you. We have the Bible. And the most comforting thing about the Bible for me is not that it has all the answers, but that it tells stories of other people in other times and other places who struggled with the same questions we struggle with. People who were confused and sad and frightened because of what they saw around them. Sometimes they even thought that God had deserted them. I bet a lot of people in Louisiana and Mississippi felt that way too.

There is, for example, a story that you might have studied in Sunday School. I just read part of it a little while ago. Do you remember how Moses led the Hebrew people to escape from slavery and Pharaoh, and how scared they were because they thought Pharaoh's army would kill them? But God saved them at the Red Sea?

And then they got to the wilderness and couldn't drink the water because it was sour and they complained, thought they were going to die? But God provided water for them?

And now they were about to die of hunger, and they started saying that they wished they were back in Egypt as slaves, because at least there they wouldn't starve? They got angry at Moses, and even God.

You see, they had forgotten all that God had done for them. They were so afraid, so into their own little lives that they forgot that God was a good God. They forgot how bad things were in Egypt in slavery, and that God had led them to freedom, and was with them, even out there in the wilderness. And then, in a way that we can't fully explain, a type of bread called "manna" appeared. Now let me tell you a little about that word "manna." In Hebrew it is actually called "man hu", which means "What is it?" And I think that helps us to see that sometimes God provides for us, but it comes in forms that we do not recognize as a gift from God. And so we see God doing some good things, but we don't notice it and we ask "What is it?"

Now I know what you're thinking, Abby. What does this have to do with Katrina and floods and suffering? Let me share a few things:

First of all, let's be careful not to blame God for everything that goes wrong. God does not want people to suffer. As a matter of fact, I think that God is suffering with us. God does not directly cause things like tsunamis (remember that last year, when thousands of people were swept away into the sea?), or hurricanes. They arise according to nature's design.

41

Indeed, if anyone is to blame for so much of the misery and devastation following Katrina, we have to look at ourselves. That's right, Abby. I'm not simply talking about you and me, I'm talking about our nation and its values, and its policies.

As I looked at the pictures and heard the stories and silently wept over them, I began to ask some other questions, questions that did not so much have to do with God, but with ourselves and our nation:

Why, in the richest nation in the history of the human race, have we allowed the kind of poverty we have seen to exist in our country? I have found out, Abby, that just about everyone who died as a result of the hurricane and the flood or was left behind, was poor or sick, or elderly. Why do we have the highest poverty rate in the developed world? Do you know that when I was your age, 10 years old, people living in poverty made up over 23 percent of our population, and we as a nation started to work on that so that only 5 years ago it had dropped to about 10 percent? But last year for the first time in 50 years, we actually saw an increase in poverty? And until the flood, I, and most Americans, I think, weren't aware of that. Most of us had grown tired of talking about poverty. Why? Maybe that's the kind of question that you and I, and others in the church can begin to ask. Like your question about God, I don't have the answer. But let's start asking those kinds of questions.

I will say this, and that is that every Thursday evening I and others are given a gift. Because I go down to the T.K. Young Room and see the room filled with people who are very different from me. They are poor, and we feed them. Why do I say this is a gift? Because I am reminded that the poor are children of God. I talk with them and eat with them. They are no less children of God than you and me. I am also given a weekly reminder that poor people are not just "out there" as "an issue" to deal with, but that they exist in our country, right here in our midst. I need to be reminded of that. And just between you and me, Abby, there are times when I would just as soon not go down there! But they're a gift because Jesus reminded us that if we feed the hungry, we feed him. If we care for the poor, we care for him. It just might be that when we look at those pictures of flood victims (like this one on Newsweek), we might see Jesus. I wonder if we truly believed what Jesus said, how that might change our nation's priorities.

So rather than blaming God, maybe Katrina will give us an opportunity to look at ourselves and starting doing all we can to make sure that this won't happen again.

There are other questions that I'm asking, like "When civil engineers studied the levees and warned that they needed fixing because they could break in a flood, why didn't our government act?" Or, "Are the scientists right when they say that the force of a hurricane can increase because of global warming?" The point I want to make is: The questions I raise are not about God, but about ourselves.

Secondly, I hope that all of the sadness and fear we feel as a result of Katrina will not blind us to all the good that God is doing. God did not cause Katrina, but God is at work in the loving and compassionate responses of people who did so much to help victims and relieve suffering. The people in the wilderness were so caught up in misery that they forgot how good God was.

Let me give you just a few examples. Abby, did you know that the Idlewild congregation alone raised over $25,000 to send to Presbyterian Disaster Relief, all of which went directly to the victims? Or that we went in together with Temple Israel and Holy Communion to raise over $40,000 in one day for the Red Cross? Or that when we were needed down in Baton Rouge with some supplies, it took only two hours for us to fill a bus with emergency needs, and three of our members went down there on one days' notice to deliver the goods and help transport people who needed medical care? Doctors, social workers, hotel owners, home and apartment owners, all offered their services.

I could tell you story after story of the lives that were touched by the gifts of this congregation. On the day we were out on Union Avenue collecting money, a number of evacuees came by to thank us; others needed help…gas to get to Atlanta, school supplies for twin daughters in the first grade in their new school, food, a place to say. We were able to help them, Abby, not just because people poured out their hearts and wallets on that day. It happened because last fall people in this congregation pledged their money to support the mission of the church. And this is part of our mission.

And even children your age have helped. On the Tuesday before the big collection day, my study door was open and I heard some giggling down the hallway. And there at my door appeared two children with a big bag full of ice cream cups from TCBY. They said they were there to "help the people who were helping people." That meant a lot to us, and I'd tell you their names but I haven't talked with them to ask their permission. So I'll just tell you that their initials are Frances and Phillip Jones.

And of course God has been working not only through Idlewild or other congregations or Memphis or even our nation. Nepal, one of the poorest nations in the world, pledged $25,000. Countries that we have treated poorly in the past, like El Salvador, pledged aid. In the midst of the suffering, let's not forget how God touches hearts, inspiring the goodness of people's response to one another. You've heard me say it over and over, "God is good, all the time. All the time, God is good."

So Abby, let's continue to ask those hard questions, not only about God, but about ourselves and our nation. I must warn you, that some people will not like hearing hard questions about God and will try to give you easy answers. Perhaps even more people will not like you asking hard questions about our nation. But because you and I are children of a God who desires that no one suffer, who gives plenty for all if only we would disperse it wisely and compassionately, question we must.

So we question, we pray, we study, we work. I pledge to you that I am going to work harder than ever, not only to help the victims of Katrina, but to reverse our nation's priorities so that they reflect the kind of love and justice that God desires for our nation and world. Maybe, with God's help, we can change the way we all live now.

But above all, let us never forget to give thanks to God, who has not only given us water to drink and bread to eat, but also has given us the Bread of Life whom we call Jesus Christ, given so that we might be forgiven, healed, liberated, and filled with goodness and light.

"What is it?" we ask when we are frightened or saddened or confused. Look more closely. It is the goodness of God breaking out all around us. Praise God from whom all blessings flow.

Thanks again for writing. I love you.

Dr. Steve

God, and Love, and Doing Things for Folks

November 9, 2014

Matthew 25:1-13

"Then the kingdom of heaven will be like this. Ten bridesmaids took their lamps and went to meet the bridegroom. 2Five of them were foolish, and five were wise. 3When the foolish took their lamps, they took no oil with them; 4but the wise took flasks of oil with their lamps. 5As the bridegroom was delayed, all of them became drowsy and slept. 6But at midnight there was a shout, 'Look! Here is the bridegroom! Come out to meet him.' 7Then all those bridesmaids got up and trimmed their lamps. 8The foolish said to the wise, 'Give us some of your oil, for our lamps are going out.' 9But the wise replied, 'No! there will not be enough for you and for us; you had better go to the dealers and buy some for yourselves.' 10And while they went to buy it, the bridegroom came, and those who were ready went with him into the wedding banquet; and the door was shut. 11Later the other bridesmaids came also, saying, 'Lord, lord, open to us.' 12But he replied, 'Truly I tell you, I do not know you.' 13Keep awake therefore, for you know neither the day nor the hour.

Prayer: Lord, to whom shall we go? You have the words of eternal life. By the mysterious power of the Holy Spirit, speak to us of your promises that we might hear your truth and enjoy you forever. Amen.

EW HUMAN EVENTS ARE MORE WEIGHTED emotionally than weddings. Parents invest heavily—time, money, energy, creativity, money, resources, love, hope, money—in the marriage ceremony for a beloved daughter or son. Because they are so loaded with emotional content, weddings are actually fragile events, with lots of potential for mishap, even disaster. Actually, even the smallest of bumps can feel like a disaster of earthquake proportions.

For one thing, almost all the characters—the bride, the groom, and their parents, not to mention the wedding party and the parents of the flower girls and ring bearers—are stretched thin, and deep feelings come easily to the surface. There are tears at weddings, and profound hope, but also, because everyone wants it to be perfect, sometimes anger, resentment, frustration with an underlying anxiety. In the midst of all of that, things can go wrong, and often do. One of the favorite pastimes of clergy is to share stories, "war stories," if you will, of wedding near-disasters: the best man got lost and didn't make it to the rehearsal; the bridal dress that tore the morning of; the bridesmaid that fainted; the flowers that didn't get delivered; the ring bearer that pitched a major hissy fit midway down the aisle; not to mention the mother of the bride who wore the lowest cut, skimpiest dress this side of the Grizzly Girls because she wanted her ex-husband to see that she "still had it." A little tension there.

But it has always been so, at least in the Judeo-Christian tradition. It is no accident, I am convinced, that the very first miracle that Jesus performed was at a wedding, changing water to wine. Something went wrong. Embarrassment, tensions, finger pointing. And Jesus made things right, and the party went on, with the very best wine.

47

But it is also significant that near the end of his life, at the time for summing up, Jesus chose this most human, emotionally loaded event as the context for a parable about the kingdom. "The kingdom of heaven will be like this." Last week we heard the preamble to Matthew's Gospel in the Beatitudes, his first sermon. "This is what the kingdom is like." Blessed are the meek. Blessed are those who mourn. Blessed are the peacemakers." This week, we hear his final "lecture," in this entire chapter, Matthew 25. It gives the disciples their marching orders.

Now, it helps to know about the wedding customs of the day. Weddings in Jesus' day were every bit as emotionally freighted as ours today, with the same potential for mishap (Like running out of wine!) Guests assembled at the home of the bride and were entertained by her parents while waiting for the groom. When the bridegroom approached, the guests, including the bridesmaids, lighted torches and went out to greet him. In a festive procession, the entire party walked to the groom's home where his parents were waiting for the ceremony and the extended banquet that would follow and continue for several days.

In this parable, for whatever reason, the groom does not show up on time; we aren't told why, but the hours pass, and many of the waiting wedding party fall asleep. Finally, at midnight, they are awakened with a shout, "He's coming!" The bridesmaids leap into action, trim their lamps and head out to meet him. But five of the ten have used up their oil and have no reserves. Their attempt to borrow some from their wiser, more prudent sisters is rejected. (One would hope that the "wiser and more prudent" sisters would have been more gracious, but they weren't. There's probably a reason, which I'll get to in a minute.) Frantically, they set out in search of oil, not an easy task at midnight, unless, I suppose you are in New York

City! And in the process, they miss the whole procession. You can just imagine the parents about to explode! When they finally arrive at the groom's home, they are locked out and dismissed. "Keep awake," Jesus concludes, "You do not know the day or the hour." Staying alert, waiting purposefully, being prepared, is the message here.

But the question is, why would Matthew put this toward the end of his gospel? He's the only gospel writer to include it. One reason might be that even early on, Matthew knew that the church was a mixed bag. Five bridesmaids were wise, five were foolish. That's the church. "Not everyone who says 'Lord, Lord,' will enter the kingdom of heaven, but only the one who does the will of my Father in heaven," Jesus said earlier in Matthew. Matthew sees the church as a field where the weeds and wheat are all mixed together. And he discouraged the zealous weeders (like the scribes and the Pharisees) who would clean up things prematurely and according to their own lights.)

But there was another reason Matthew put it here. This was written 50, maybe 60 years after Jesus' death, resurrection, and ascension. They had been waiting and waiting and waiting for Jesus to return. Paul, who wrote a little earlier, was faced with the same problem. The early church was beginning to struggle with what it meant to experience the absence of Jesus, and not just his presence. Jesus hadn't returned like they had expected, so what were they to do in the meantime? "Watch." "Keep awake." "Stay alert." And in the meantime, live faithfully, courageously, hopefully. And that is our mission still.

At the heart of our faith is the certainty that human history has a purpose and a goal that is moving toward eventual fulfillment and completion. We mainstream Presbyterians don't talk about that a lot, don't articulate it very well, and even avoid it because of its abuse by popular end-of-timers like Tim LeHaye in his Left Behind series, who sell lots of books, very unbiblical books by the way, describing the end of history in graphic and (mostly) violent terms and who focus on the end times to the neglect of this time, this world.

That's not the point of this parable. The point is living expectantly and hopefully. Christian hope rests on trust that the God who created the whole world will continue to love the world with gentle providence, will continue the process of creation until the project is complete, and will continue to redeem and save the world by coming into it with love and grace, in Jesus Christ.

Christian hope is as big as the whole sweep of history. "The arc of the universe is long, but it bends towards justice," as Dr. King reminded us. Good news for many of us. But it is also as small as each individual. I don't know if any of you have ever heard of Sadie Virginia Thompson. Miss Sadie lived in Johnston Falls, West Virginia, which was also the home of the Laurel Literary Society. It was THE way to climb the social ladder. And Sadie wanted to belong. She really wanted to, asked about it, but she was never asked to join because, well, she made her living sewing and her father worked at the factory and she lived on the wrong side of the tracks. Her mother had died, and Sadie had never married because she had to look after her father.

In 1914, 100 years ago, after Sadie had saved up for years, she was able to realize her dream to visit Europe. Took a big ocean liner over there, but arrived just as World War I was breaking out. She got stranded in Belgium and tried to make a dash for Paris but somehow got lost, and ended up wandering around a field where there had obviously just been a battle. She heard a wounded soldier moan, offered him water and began to care for him and for a few other wounded men. She stayed among them all night, giving them water, binding their wounds, tearing her shirt to make bandages, singing to them.

When she was finally able to return to Johnston Falls, she told a friend, "I'd never known what it was to have children, but that night all of those men were my children, even the biggest and roughest of them. And I believe I could have died for any one of them."

Well, word got out about the work she did there, and she was approached by a friend. "Well, you'll be pleased to know that the Laurel Literary Society will be glad to have you belong to it now!" But Sadie replied, "Oh, you don't understand. I've been face to face with death and hell and God. Do you reckon any of those old things matter now?"

Her friend was taken aback. "What does matter?" she asked. Sadie said "Nothing! Nothing! Nothing but God and love and doing things for folks."

Sadie was right. She sounded a lot like the prophet Micah, didn't she, who said nothing matters…nothing! Except doing justice, loving kindness, and walking humbly with God.

In every congregation, including this one, there are people genuinely frightened about where human history seems to be headed. I have my moments. Freedom, justice, and compassion seem so …fragile…in the faces of oppression, injustice, violence. Living in hope doesn't mean immunity from the harsh realities of history. On the contrary, it means living confidently and expectantly; trusting that the Lord of history continues to come into life with compassion and redemption and hope.

The challenge is to keep enough oil on hand for the lamps when the bridegroom appears, to roll up sleeves and work for the kingdom that is always coming and breaking into history.

And in every congregation, including this one, people are genuinely afraid for their own personal future, perhaps facing serious illness, surgery, the loss of employment, issues with children. They, and each of us, need to hear the good news that the bridegroom will come, that the love of God will continue to appear in our lives in surprising and unexpected ways:

> --Jesus Christ comes when Christian people live in hope and never give up.
> --Jesus Christ comes when faithful disciples express love and compassion and work for justice.
> --Jesus Christ comes when critically ill people know they are ultimately safe in God's love.
> --Heaven breaks into earth when faithful women and men live in hope and give themselves to the work of the kingdom.

And if we live our lives with that kind of expectancy, that kind of hope, that kind of courage, then we become free for all time to get on with those things that really matter. We don't have to spend all that time in angst, worrying about so many of those things we worry about. We don't have to decide who is in and who is out; who the wheat is and who the weeds are.

I hope you'll notice that during our stewardship campaign, we didn't claim that pledging, making a commitment to support the ministry of this church, was about earning a place in the kingdom, or setting us above those who don't. It was out of sheer gratitude, with glad and generous hearts…that that grace is sufficient of us, and surely more than we deserve.

God and love and doing things for folks. That's what we are about, is it not? God and love and doing things for folks. Like teaching children, hugging older folks, walking with people through the valley of the shadow of death, loving the sometimes unlovable; listening, really listening to the pain of those who have been hurt by the church, preparing meals for the sick, praying together, working for justice, planting a garden, baptizing children, and building a church that is as just and generous as God's grace.

So wait, stay awake, and prepare by doing those things that really matter: God and love and doing things for folks.

Houses Don't Stay Empty

January 1, 2012
(New Year's Day)

Matthew 12:34-35

34You brood of vipers! How can you speak good things, when you are evil? For out of the abundance of the heart the mouth speaks. 35The good person brings good things out of a good treasure, and the evil person brings evil things out of an evil treasure.

Prayer: You are the God who makes all things new. So on this first day of a new year, we ask that you will make these old scriptures new to us, so we might be startled once again into the extravagant, boundless love you have for all your children. And may the words of my mouth and the meditations of our hearts be acceptable in your sight, O Lord, our strength and our redeemer. Amen.

ONCE UPON A TIME," SAID JESUS, "THERE WAS man possessed by a demon, an evil spirit. This demon had set up housekeeping in the man's soul. It had the run of the man's life."

Thus begins one of the shortest stories Jesus told. If you and I heard someone start to tell a story with those words, we might dismiss it as a fable of old, an affront to our enlightened thinking. Demons? Evil spirits? Ha!

But if we would have been there that day when Jesus spoke, I think we might have noticed a hush settling in over the crowd. He was addressing the Pharisees, that is, the good religious people of the day…. (The elders, the deacons, the Sunday school teachers, the preachers, maybe even a few choir members), who strained forward. The curious knot of on-lookers tightened, for in those days, belief in demons was widespread. People pictured the universe in layers. God dwelt in a realm of calm, above the sky. People dwelt on the earth. But in between was the demon-filled air. A person's most fearful foes were not those that he could see. They were the powers of darkness—the devils and demons. So when Jesus began his story, his audience did not scoff or poke fun at him. They listened.

"This demon controlled the man's life," said Jesus. "It made his existence miserable. SO he engaged the demon in battle and after quite a struggle, he cast the demon out." He thought he was free. Isn't that the picture? "I've kicked the devil out---now I'm free!" "With the demon gone, the man began to tidy up his soul. He swept it. He polished and buffed it. He made it beautiful, rearranged it, saying to himself, "Now I'll have peace for I've gotten rid of the demon. What a bright, clean, shining soul I have." "Well," said Jesus, "this evicted demon went on a trip. It visited many places, saw many things. But after wandering around for a while, it grew increasingly homesick for the old surroundings. "I think I'll go back and have a look at the old flat," said the demon. "So it returned."

Now, of course, it immediately noted the change. Things had been tidied up. On tiptoe, the demon peeked through the windows of the man's soul. It was pleased to find that the place had been re-decorated. It was bright and cheerful and very orderly. But the demon noted something else which set its heart to racing. It saw that the man had been so busy dusting and polishing and organizing his

55

soul that he'd neglected to engage a new tenant. The house was empty—sterile, but empty. So that demon decided to slip back in. But as it thought about it, the demon came to this conclusion: "I can't go back into such a fine place all alone. That's too comfortable a set-up for just one, small demon. I'll go out and round up a few of my pals." So it raced off to a near-by hangout, found seven buddies and said, "Come with me, fellows, I've found a place to crash." And together, they gushed into the man's life." Jesus ended his parable by saying that the man's last condition was worse than his first.

Now why did Jesus tell such a story to the religious leaders of his day, to those people who were so careful to keep the law? What did it mean?

Well, these religious people believed that they had cleansed their lives of wrong. According to their way of thinking they had kicked the devil out. As a result, they had nothing better to do than to spend their days in polishing their souls. They were careful of what they ate, of what they wore. They made sure that they said just the right number of prayers, that the hem of their cloak was just the right length. They made sure they associated with the right kind of people—the pure; and kept their distance from those who were not considered "pure." And in various ways they let other people know of their goodness. In other words, they basked in the sterile quality of their souls.

But Jesus said to them, and oh how it must have cut, "The trouble with you good, decent religious folk is that you have spent so much time sanitizing your souls that you've overlooked God. You haven't any time for your fellow human beings. You've been so busy polishing, that you've created a vacuum. As a result, pride and self-satisfaction and self-righteousness and bigotry have captured your soul. So actually, you're in worse shape now than you were before you got religion!"

Now, that's what Jesus was saying to the Pharisees, but it seems to me that this parable—which isn't even in the lectionary—has something to say to us today, in light of the beginning of a new year. What do I mean? Well, it's no secret that at this time of the year many of us make resolutions. We may not have told our neighbors, or our families about them, but some of us have determined to kind of clean up our lives—to make a fresh start. This parable warns us in advance to be on guard in our reformation. For the danger of change—that is, reforming our behavior and our attitudes and our habits—is that we'll fall into the same kind of trap that ensnared the Pharisees.

Let me share with you what I mean through a rather personal example. In a former church, I met a fellow who had a demon— this particular demon was an illness called alcoholism. I got to know him over some cups of coffee, and we got to the point where we could actually talk about his problem that he was having—talk about how it had already cost him a good job, how it was undermining his marriage. Well, this man, with a great deal of outside support, finally shook the habit. He recognized he was hooked, got treatment, joined A.A. and stopped drinking. He kicked the demon out. His life was cleansed. He joined a church, telling me on more occasions that I can remember how he was "saved." He never missed a service. But then something happened. He became proud of his good conduct, of his virtue, proud in a vicious way. He became the self-appointed judge over the community. He lost his warmth, his compassion. He had no time for others who were caught. In short, he became a self-righteous bore. His whole attitude was "I picked myself up and am clean. Others should do the same."

Now heaven knows we don't want to fall into the trap of Pharisaic judgmentalism and judge this man. You have to be careful with a story like this; you have to continue to love him, even if you don't like him, but do you see what happened? Though the one demon had been evicted, this fellow had become so proud and self-righteous and so judgmental that his last condition was worse than his first. He was a man that people avoided.

What I'm suggesting is that this story that Jesus told isn't make believe. It has within it a principle of life and we see the principle brought to light all around us. The counselor, for example, may cast out the fears which infect a life. He or she may, through their gifts and competence, release a soul from the plague of an inferiority complex, but unless something positive moves in to take the place of that evicted complex, a more serious illness may overtake that life. I mean, a confident selfishness or a bigoted egoism is poor salvation for an inferiority complex!

And we see this in the wider areas of life. We can tear down old projects that have become havens of crime and poverty and drugs and replace them with nice park-like developments; we can clean and polish old communities, but unless we take a look at the deeper issues that caused poverty in the first place, unless we use our resources to strengthen a new educational system with mutual respect and responsibility standing by to take over, it is wasted effort. You see, it is a principle of life. Houses don't stay empty.

Reformation, in itself, is never enough. We must be careful as to who moves in after the rascals have been kicked out or we might discover that our last condition is worse than our first. The world thought that the defeat of the Kaiser would create a new Germany and solve the riddle of war, but after Germany was defeated, the house was left empty. Hitlerism arrived with 7 other "devils." Anti-Semitism, the scientific contempt of life.

So it is with us. Troubled by our failings, our disappointments, our sins, both overt and covert over the past year, we vow resolutions at the start of a new year. The devils which tear and befoul our lives can no longer be endured. So we determine to kick the rascals out. We begin careful reform. We draw up a list of resolutions; the house is cleansed, we say; swept clean of its worst defilements. But how often it is left empty. It's never enough simply to make resolutions. Something has to take the place of that which is discarded.

So what can that be? Now, this is going to sound like preacher talk, but I want to suggest, with all the persuasion that I can muster that if you want an exhilarating year, a year which will set before you some crisis situations which will test your metal, or some hum-drum ordinariness which will lull you to apathy, try filling your life with the words and the teachings—above all the attitudes, of that Man of Galilee, for I am convinced that it is he who has given us the clue as to what it means to be human. In your friendships, in your relationships, on the job where ethical decisions do not come easily, in the political stands which the corporate nature of our lives demand—in those situations where you are under terrific pressure to conform—try putting into practice the kind of enthusiastic, exuberant love for life which was characterized by Christ and I promise you a hear of adventure.

Now, please notice that I've stressed the words exhilaration and adventure. I'm not suggesting that you'll have a year of good feelings, an easy year, a year of roses, a year without lumps, because it won't take you long to discover that as soon as you begin to take his demands seriously, as soon as you try to apply with your lives those things that so many people applaud with their lips –like an insistence on justice; a plea for peace and an end to war; like a humane treatment of immigrants and others; like a fair and equitable school system; like truth-telling from our leaders; as soon as you really demonstrate your commitment to the Man Jesus, you're going to be in hot water. You'll get flack, especially if you dare to suggest that Jesus might have something to say about the economic and political priorities which shape our society. Or the ecological adjustment which might result through a cut-back in corporate profits.

But yes, I can promise a year of adventure—if only your enthusiasm holds out. That's the one thing that Pharisees can't tolerate: our enthusiasm; our commitment to the principles of life and not death….the joy of freedom.

No, it's not simply enough to reform, we've got to re-form to something better. And therein is the parable. Devils possess the home which invites no worthier tenant.

And I can't think of a better place to begin the re-forming that coming to the Table. After all, there is room at this table for all.

My Son, My Son

August 9, 2009

II Samuel 18:5-9, 15, 31-33

5 The king ordered Joab and Abishai and Ittai, saying, "Deal gently for my sake with the young man Absalom." And all the people heard when the king gave orders to all the commanders concerning Absalom. 6 So the army went out into the field against Israel; and the battle was fought in the forest of Ephraim. 7 The men of Israel were defeated there by the servants of David, and the slaughter there was great on that day, twenty thousand men. 8 The battle spread over the face of all the country; and the forest claimed more victims that day than the sword.

9 Absalom happened to meet the servants of David. Absalom was riding on his mule, and the mule went under the thick branches of a great oak. His head caught fast in the oak, and he was left hanging between heaven and earth, while the mule that was under him went on.

15 And ten young men, Joab's armor-bearers, surrounded Absalom and struck him, and killed him.

31 Then the Cushite came; and the Cushite said, "Good tidings for my lord the king! For the Lord has vindicated you this day, delivering you from the power of all who rose up against you." 32 The king said to the Cushite, "Is it well with the young man Absalom?" The Cushite answered, "May the enemies of my lord the king, and all who rise up to do you harm, be like that young man." 33 The king was deeply moved, and went up to the chamber over the gate, and wept; and as he went, he said, "O my son Absalom, my son, my son Absalom! Would I had died instead of you, O Absalom, my son, my son!"

Prayer: Gracious God, in the stillness of this moment, we remember that you are God, and that without our asking, you have fed us with the bread of life. Grant now that as we hear your words, we might be startled yet again with the renewing, refreshing, and re-generating sustenance that you have given us in your son, our Savior, Jesus Christ. Amen.

WHO NEEDS SOAP OPERAS? WHO NEEDS reality shows? We have David.

We've been following his story over the past weeks from the time he was secretly anointed by Samuel in his youth to be king. Remember how he was described as "one after God's own heart?" And then he rose to the public eye through the legendary victory over Goliath. He wrested power from Saul through his wit and cleverness and ascended to the throne of Israel and Judah. He ruled with wisdom and power.

But of course, there was his dark side. His romantic attraction to Bathsheba, whom he seized for himself, and the conspiracy he entered to kill Uriah, her husband, was certainly the low point of David's moral leadership. But the soap opera isn't over. Today we hear about family dysfunction and political intrigue and personal tragedy.

Absalom was his son, one of seven that he had with six wives. He wasn't the first born but he was the one who was most like his father, clever, bright, an opportunist who knew about political capital, where to put it and how to get it.

The first we hear of Absalom is in a sordid story of revenge. Absalom had a beautiful sister, Tamar and Absalom's half-brother, (the first born) Amnon, was lovesick for her. That lovesickness turned sour when Amnon raped Tamar.

Absalom became bent on revenge. It took two years to arrange it, but he settled the score. Absalom got Amnon drunk on a camping trip, and when the moment was right, Absalom's men pounced on his brother and killed him. It looks like Absalom learned well from his father David.

Absalom took off and went into a self-imposed exile for three years, hiding from his father's wrath. And back in Jerusalem, David mourned Amnon's death every day.

But over time David realized that all the grieving in the world could not bring Amnon back, and he simply could not bear the sorrow of the separation from his most favored son. He had already lost one son, and he missed Absalom greatly, so he sent word to Absalom to come home, just come home. You see, David loved Absalom more than words could express. And all of Israel loved him too. As the storyteller says, "…in all Israel there was no one so much to be praised for his beauty as Absalom; from the sole of his foot to the crown of his head there was no blemish in him."

But then note what the storyteller adds: "When he cut the hair of his head (for at the end of every year he used to cut it; when it was heavy on him) [it weighed] two hundred shekels by the king's weight." Remember that. There is a reason that little detail is in there.

So Absalom came back, but it wasn't like the homecoming we read about in the Prodigal Son with the father running out to greet him and throwing a party. As a matter of fact, David did not receive him, and would not even speak to him when he passed him on the street. The relationship turned to ice. And Absalom, so much like his father, began to subvert David's power. He wheeled around Jerusalem in a fashionable chariot, drawing whatever attention to himself he could. He became a favorite of the local paparazzi. And he began to think "You know, these people love me. I can do a better job at running this country than my old man."

Suffice it to say that if Barak Obama had a son and he turned out to be like Rush Limbaugh, it would have been the kind of trouble David had on his hands with Absalom. But David still loved this child of his own bosom.

Eventually Absalom decided to make his move and mounted a coup. He went off to Hebron and announced that he was king. With that move, David saw his power erode so deeply that he had to flee for his life. He left it all—power, riches, fame, palace, wives, concubines, a kingdom.

He gathers his loyalists together and raises an army. As his troops are riding off to do battle with Absalom's insurrectionists he pleads with his commanders, Joab, Abishai, and Ittai, in some of the most poignant words in all of scripture: "Deal gently for my sake with the young man Absalom." This was a father speaking, and not a king. Rebellion, disrespect, and betrayal notwithstanding, David could not ignore the blood that tied him to Absalom. Family is like that.

But the soldiers, of course, were used to ridding the nation of any threat to security. Joab was not so much moved by family compassion as he was wanting to do what was best for the king and the kingdom.

The battle was fierce, bloody and right in the midst of it, General Joab heard that Absalom had been sighted in the forest of Eprhraim. Remember the head of beautiful, long hair? It had gotten caught in a tree, and he was unable to loose himself. Joab, clearer than David about the needs of the state, decided to take matters into his own hands, and he finished off Absalom without remorse. The war ends, David's throne is re-established, and Absalom's threat is extinguished.

David went back to Jerusalem and awaited word. The messenger was ecstatic. David's kingdom is safe, his throne restored, and Israel is at peace. And, oh yes, Absalom has been killed.

What follows is a cry to heaven so loud that it will echo in every age and be heard in every family where sorrow has struck and grief has overtaken. David doesn't even hear the words of victory; all he hears is the loss of his son. His heart is fractured, he who is "one after God's own heart," and he cries as only a parent who has lost a child can cry, "O my son Absalom, my son, my son, Absalom! Would I had died instead of you, O Absalom, my son, my son." Five times he cries out the words, "my son."

There isn't a parent here who cannot empathize with the sorrow of David. Throw out all of his schemes, his adultery, his power madness, and we are with him. Because every child rebels and rejects parents in some way, some by open rebellion, some with quiet rejection of the parent's example and the modest determination to do things differently in his or her own life. Psychologists call it "individuation," and it's necessary, a good thing. Fortunately not every parent's experience of individuation is that of David's whose son rejects all that he is.

Of all the grief on earth, there is perhaps none more consuming than that of the loss of a child. It has to be the hardest of all. We all expect at some level that we will bury a parent, a husband or a wife, a sister or a brother, and we know that we ourselves must reckon with our life's end to. That's only right. But one does not expect, and our sense of rightness does not permit us to imagine that we should ever live so long as to bury a child.

That's why David's cry is so full of pathos. It is our worst nightmare, a thought we would never want to entertain for any longer than it might take to banish it. And what father or mother would not have a hundred times a hundred regrets and memories to have to absolve over time at such an untimely loss? It is no wonder that the divorce rate among parents who have lost a child is so much higher than average—the stress, the grief, the assignment of blame is that great. And so it is a terrible weight upon the soul.

I think it's a wonder that David was able to love Absalom in the way he did, with so much rejection of him in Absalom's heart. Why didn't he use what we now call "tough love?" Another father or mother might have given up at some earlier point.

Bill Muehl was my professor of preaching at Yale. A witty, eloquent, often humorous speaker, he once stopped a lecture and told of the time when their adult son called one rainy night and pleaded to come home and sleep off his high. It was the end of the line after years of this kind of thing, family torn to shreds, calls in the night, trips to the jail for bail, putting him out of the house, forcing him to live on his own, evictions from his digs, the whole bit, and Dr. Muehl said it was the hardest thing he ever had to do in his life that night to tell his son calling from a telephone booth on the other side of New Haven, "No," and hang up the phone. O Absalom, my son, my son.

I have known parents who have rejected their children on lesser grounds, turned their back on them and shut the door on them, treated their children as though they were dead, bolstered by something they convinced themselves was principle. A child rebels, gets into trouble, or becomes pregnant. I officiated at a wedding in which one set of parents did not attend because their daughter was marrying a young man of a different race. There are parents who turn their backs when their child announces he is gay, or she is lesbian. In 1985, I think it was, I did a funeral in which the parents did not show up. On his deathbed he shared with them that he had AIDS. You think that's easy to judge? I tell you, it is a decision that will tear your insides apart.

This business of being a parent is not a science but an art, and none of us is perfect at it. It is only learned through hard experience. Children break your heart just as they fill it with joy. From the moment they come into your life, you are exposed. There is the night he has the croup and you stay up all night watching him, turning the shower on hot so the steam fills his lungs. You put the salve on his chest and rock him, singing lullabies until about daybreak, and when he's finally asleep, you lay him back in the crib and it is at that point that you realize just how frightened you were. And that is just the beginning.

Now I know what you are thinking. Old man Steve is having a hard time this week taking his first born off to college. It's stirring up a lot. I plead guilty, but it's a good thing. But at times like this one does realize how exposed and how vulnerable this work is of being a father, being a mother it is disarming. It reminds me of something…

It reminds me of another son of David and of a father in heaven whose heart breaks at the hurt, the rebellion, and the suffering his children. God, who is both father and mother to us all, is better at this thing called parenting than any of us can ever hope to be, and in large part it is because God is better at being vulnerable than any of us have ever been.

I know that most of you have heard me tell the story of William Sloane Coffin at the Riverside Church in New York the week after his son drowned in Boston harbor in a car he was driving under the influence of alcohol. In words of eloquence and faith, the preacher told his congregation, "My consolation lies in knowing that it was not the will of God that Alex died; that when the waves closed over the sinking car, God's heart was the first of all our hearts to break."

Out of the depths we cry to God and discover that God is there ahead of us.

As David weeps over his lost child, he cries aloud, "Would I had died instead of you, O Absalom," an exchange David could not make, a trade no parent can effect: Save one.

For God's love for us was so great that a thousand years after David, another son was lost upon a tree, upon a cross raised above a barren hill outside Jerusalem, and heaven cried. For the kind of love God has for us is so great that God would enter into the suffering and sorrow, the grief and pain that all of us know, so that our sorrow might be known in heaven and redeemed in grace. In him, in Jesus Christ, "one after God's own heart," every cry is heard, every sorrow is known, and every grief is borne for our sake.

And as for us, we trust in God, who grieved as well the death of a son. Who takes compassion on our loneliness, has mercy on our grief, and who has given us a Savior when we cry out for all that is lost and all that is found in our lives.

"In life and in death," we say in the words of one of our creeds, "we belong to God." And at the last of David's life what else is there to say. From the great moments of his victories, to the heartbreak of his grief, the story has always been about God even more than about David. God who will not let us go. God, to whom in life and in death, we belong forever.

And in God's time, as the writer of Revelation will foresee, every tear shall be wiped away from our eyes, and death shall be no more, neither shall there be mourning nor crying nor pain any more, for the former things will have passed away.

And in Christ, at last, David's cry to heaven will be answered, "O Absalom, my son, my son."

Amen.

Lord, To Whom Can We Go?

August 23, 2009

John 6:56-69

56 Those who eat my flesh and drink my blood abide in me, and I in them. 57 Just as the living Father sent me, and I live because of the Father, so whoever eats me will live because of me. 58 This is the bread that came down from heaven, not like that which your ancestors ate, and they died. But the one who eats this bread will live forever." 59 He said these things while he was teaching in the synagogue at Capernaum.

60 When many of his disciples heard it, they said, "This teaching is difficult; who can accept it?" 61 But Jesus, being aware that his disciples were complaining about it, said to them, "Does this offend you? 62 Then what if you were to see the Son of Man ascending to where he was before? 63 It is the spirit that gives life; the flesh is useless. The words that I have spoken to you are spirit and life. 64 But among you there are some who do not believe." For Jesus knew from the first who were the ones that did not believe, and who was the one that would betray him. 65 And he said, "For this reason I have told you that no one can come to me unless it is granted by the Father." 66 Because of this many of his disciples turned back and no longer went about with him. 67 So Jesus asked the twelve, "Do you also wish to go away?" 68 Simon Peter answered him, "Lord, to whom can we go? You have the words of eternal life. 69 We have come to believe and know that you are the Holy One of God."

Prayer: We praise you, O God, for all the mystery of life, for work well done, for hard choices that help us discover who we are, and above all, for the gift of faith that makes your love in Christ the sure foundation on which we build our lives. Allow us now to hear what we need to hear, so that we may be able to do what you would have us do, through Jesus Christ our Lord. Amen.

P RESBYTERIANS GENERALLY AREN'T BIG ON testimonies. You know, where individuals get up and talk, often passionately about how they claimed Jesus as their Lord and Savior and the difference that made in their lives, sometimes leading to genuine change on a deep level, sometimes claiming that their decision for Christ was responsible for a financial windfall, and sometimes in the more Pentecostal churches, getting caught up in tongues of the Holy Spirit.

Presbyterians aren't big on testimonies. For one thing, we are a more reserved people. "God's frozen chosen," we have been called. But there is also a theological reason, for our tradition, beginning with John Calvin himself, places ultimate emphasis not on our making a decision for Christ, but on God's making a decision for us in Christ. That is not to say that our choice is unimportant. It is to say that our choice comes second, because it is God who elects, God who chooses; indeed, I would go so far as to say that God alone makes it possible for us at some point in our lives to stand and confess, along with Simon Peter in today's text, that we have come to believe and know the "Holy One of God."

We cannot take a bit of credit for it, but can only receive the gift of faith with gratitude, and that forms the basis of all that we do. Gratitude. Whatever it means to be a Christian today, it means not being arrogant and puffing up one's own chest and saying, "I am a born-again Christian, and if you are not, then I feel very sorry for you." It takes a certain amount of humility.

Now, I give you all of that as a preface for me to give a bit of personal testimony. I am going against the advice of all of my homiletics professors, and if you hear a rumble it is John Calvin turning over in his grave, wherever it is. No one knows to this day. He asked to be buried in an unmarked grave because he did not believe that the focus should be on him, nor anyone else, but on God. But there are two events that converge to lead me to do this. The first is our text today, which has been one of the most significant ones in my own personal spiritual development through the years. But the other took place this past week, or to be more accurate, took place 40 years ago this past week. You probably read about it. There were specials on TV. There is a movie coming out soon. I am speaking, of course, about Woodstock. It has brought back a lot of memories.

Oh, I wasn't there. I was working a summer job getting ready for college. (One person who is very near and dear to me, my bride of 32 years, was there!) But I really didn't hear about it much until I arrived in college a few weeks later.

But all of these retrospectives on Woodstock have taken me back to those days, and if you have been paying attention, Woodstock wasn't the only significant event to take place that summer. Just a few weeks earlier, we had placed a man on the moon. Just a few days later, Charles Manson and his followers committed their grisly murders. The Stonewall riots in New York took place in the summer of '69. Cities were burning. The Viet Nam war was at its height. And we were all still living with the repercussions of the long hot summer of 1968. The assassination of Martin Luther King. The assassination of Robert Kennedy. The riots at the Democratic Convention in Chicago. More riots in Newark and Watts and Detroit and elsewhere.

And I went off to college 40 years ago next week. I wasn't a rebel or anything like that. Some rebelled by doing drugs or alcohol. I rebelled by going north to college. It was a small thing, but a step

72

towards individuation from my culture and my family, all of whom were products of the south and southern colleges. Oh, it was a small, safe, Presbyterian liberal arts college, but still … I'd be cavorting with Yankees!

And when I went I had no intention of having anything to do with the church. It wasn't just because I was burnt out from being there when the church doors were open. It was more because I began to feel that the church had nothing to say. All of this was going on in our nation and our world, and I never once remember any of this being addressed from the pulpit or Sunday school, or even forums. The church was silent. A whole younger generation was searching for meaning, for something which I could not even define, asking questions of ultimate significance, challenging worn out values, and the church had nothing to say.

In my first week of orientation, I heard Ray Swartzback speak. Swartzy was the pastor of the church on campus, and he captivated me in a way no one ever had. He was an older man (about the age I am now!), and had until recently always served inner city, African American churches, even though he was white. He had taken on much of their suffering. I remember him telling me of taking his youth group from Cincinnati to an amusement park. This was back in the 50's. "All are welcome," the advertisement said. And so he scraped up enough money to be able to take his kids there. They were so excited. They had never done anything like this. And they got there, and it turns out all were not welcome. They had to turn around and go back. He was at Wooster because his church in Detroit had burned down during those riots I mentioned earlier.

Swartzy was a veteran of World War II and saw firsthand what war did to the soul of a person and nation. He came home from the war, went to seminary and felt that Jesus meant it when he said "Blessed are the peacemakers." And yet I don't believe to this day I have ever met anyone more full of joy. And so I wanted to hear more. I'd get up most, not all, Sunday mornings and walk over to the chapel in my jeans and sandals and hear him. And one of the first sermons I heard was on this text we have before us today. "Lord, to whom can we go?" And ever since, that question has been at the forefront of my journey.

Swartzy reminded us that Jesus had been very popular. Crowds would gather around him by the thousands. And even back then, before inclusivity became such a buzzword, the good pastor painted pictures of the wide variety of people who were eager to hear what he had to say...from tax collectors to fishermen, from little children to women, from public officials to lepers, from poor folks to people with means.

But it was Swartzy's contention that this text was one of the most critical in all of Jesus' ministry. For they began to fall away. Maybe they followed Jesus for the wrong reasons. He had just fed over 5,000 people and he began to sense that they were only interested in feeding their stomachs. "You came to me because you wanted bread, not because you sought me," he said.

And Jesus then gave one of his difficult sayings. (Of course, I'd be hard pressed to find any saying of Jesus that wasn't difficult!) He spoke of the need for people to eat his flesh and drink his blood, saying, in effect, that if we are to grasp what he is all about, then we must absorb his teaching—we must feed on him until his mind becomes our mind, until his compassion and concern becomes our compassion and concern.

That sounds simple to us, because we have had 2,000 years to think about it. But put yourselves in the place of those who were there that day, hearing these words for the first time. They were looking for a place on earth; he was talking about a place in heaven. They were looking for food for their stomachs; he was talking about food for their soul. His words were too fuzzy, too vague. He talked too much of love, too much of peace, so they turned away. "The disciples turned back," John tells us, "and no longer went about with him." There were now only twelve.

It had to hurt, being rejected by those whom he loved. And he asked perhaps the most poignant question in all the Bible. "And you, do you also wish to go away?" Were their tears in his eyes as he asked it? It had to hurt.

Well, as we know, the answer came from Peter, Peter the rugged outdoorsman, a fisherman, who answered with the simplicity of a child with another question, "Lord, to whom can we go?" Peter is saying that we have to turn to something....to someone...if we turn away. There must be something by which to live. So where do we go when we turn him off?

Don't you wonder where they went that day? They had to turn somewhere, to something, someone, when they turned away. Maybe some went back to their families and businesses, devoting their all, their mind, body and soul to the corporate monolith that told them who they were, devoting 60, 80, 100 hours a week.

Maybe they turned back and went back to their old way of doing things, just trying to get ahead. Maybe some turned away and turned within themselves, floating in fear of others, finding a personal, "Me and God" kind of religion. I'll bet some turned to a spiritual cafeteria, grazing on a little of this and a little of that to satisfy their fancy. Heaven knows, there have always been a lot of spiritual dishes being served, some of which have some value, others of which can be destructive.

I'll bet some turned back to the comfortable confines of their former religion and way of life. A religion which was safe, non-threatening, didn't upset Caesar. They didn't want a rabbi meddling in those affairs.

I remember Fred Craddock telling the story of the time some years ago in Germany when he was riding a train and struck up a conversation with a kindly middle aged woman traveling in the same compartment. "Oh, so you're a preacher," she said after they got to know each other a little. "Yes, I am." "I don't go to church," she said. "Want to know why?" He had heard just about every reason under the sun why people didn't go to church, but he didn't want to be rude, so he pastorally said, "Why?"

"Have you ever heard of the S.S.?" she asked. "Oh yes," he responded. "My father was in the S.S.," she told him. "He was a dutiful S.S. officer. And as far as I know he never missed a Sunday in church … never had a twinge … as far as I know he never heard a sermon that would give him the slightest inclination that there was any contradiction between following Hitler and following Jesus. No, I don't go to church. The church has nothing to say."

It's my guess that those people that deserted Jesus that day probably heard very clearly what he had to say, and they knew at some point, a decision would have to be made about whom they would have to place their ultimate confidence in. And they went back to their safe, comfortable confines of their religion.

When we turn away from Jesus, we have to turn somewhere. It's very interesting to note how Peter phrased the question. He didn't say "Where do we go?" "What do we go to?" He was smarter than that. He was wise enough to see that our really basic needs are not met my abstract ideas, even words like love and mercy and humility and compassion, but that it takes a relationship. The really basic needs are met in relation to the One who brings love and joy and freedom to life.

And so for forty years, ever since I first heard that question raised, I've asked that question to myself over and over again. "Steve, do you also wish to go away?" It sure has been tempting at times. I get tired of the church conflicts, the politics of it all, the long hours, the trappings of religion, the hurts; I get tired of the way fundamentalists have taken Jesus out of his context, removed his very humanity, and have made him into something he never was. I get tired of Christians who use the bible as a weapon. And so I look around. There really are a lot of alternatives, you know. But I end up with the same question that Peter responded with. The same question that was posed by Swartzy, "To whom can we go?"

In the last sermon I heard Swartzy preach before he left Wooster and went back to Cleveland to serve in an inner city church there, he told the story of the time Leonardo da Vinci was about to finish his famous painting of the Last Supper. He invited his students to come in and take a look at it and critique it. He unveiled it and the students praised the intricate work, beauty and delicacy of—the tablecloth. The legend is the Leonardo took a brush with paint and with one sweeping gesture painted over the tablecloth. "You fools," he said. "Look at the Master's face. Look at the Master's face!"

What I have seen over and over again is that we worship a God who has shown us the very face of God. Yes, I was a Christian by birth, but I became a Christian, and remain a Christian because I began to discover about forty years ago a road, a road less traveled to be sure, but a road that went beyond dogmas and neat divisions of humanity and sheep and goats. If I were asked to name it, I would say it's called grace. If I were asked who built it, I would say Jesus, the Jewish teacher, whom Christian call the Christ.

So friends, I would like to hold up to all of you—all of you—first-timers here, the hangers-on, the pillars of the church, the seekers, the students, the young people—everyone. I would like to hold up to you the One who can bring love and freedom and joy to life. The one who can satisfy our deepest longing.

Following him is the greatest adventure and highest calling any of us might have in life. I must warn you: His words are not always easy. His teachings are difficult. His requirements demanding. But he didn't just teach and live and love and give us words. He gave us himself. He is the One who is the Living Water, poured out for us; Living Bread, broken for our sake.

And if we choose to follow him, we too might be poured out, and broken. But I have found that it is the way to the fullness of life, what he called eternal life.

I invite you to consider the alternatives, and hope that you too might answer the way Peter answered, "Lord, to whom can we go?"

And who knows, when we answer that, the world just might find that the church has something to say.

Amen.

Just Words
March 27, 2011

John 4:1-30, 39-42

Now when Jesus learned that the Pharisees had heard, "Jesus is making and baptizing more disciples than John" 2—although it was not Jesus himself but his disciples who baptized— 3he left Judea and started back to Galilee.

4But he had to go through Samaria. 5So he came to a Samaritan city called Sychar, near the plot of ground that Jacob had given to his son Joseph. 6Jacob's well was there, and Jesus, tired out by his journey, was sitting by the well. It was about noon. 7A Samaritan woman came to draw water, and Jesus said to her, "Give me a drink." 8(His disciples had gone to the city to buy food.) 9The Samaritan woman said to him, "How is it that you, a Jew, ask a drink of me, a woman of Samaria?" (Jews do not share things in common with Samaritans.) 10Jesus answered her, "If you knew the gift of God, and who it is that is saying to you, 'Give me a drink,' you would have asked him, and he would have given you living water." 11The woman said to him, "Sir, you have no bucket, and the well is deep. Where do you get that living water? 12Are you greater than our ancestor Jacob, who gave us the well, and with his sons and his flocks drank from it?" 13Jesus said to her, "Everyone who drinks of this water will be thirsty again, 14but those who drink of the water that I will give them will never be thirsty. The water that I will give will become in them a spring of water gushing up to eternal life." 15The woman said to him, "Sir, give me this water, so that I may never be thirsty or have to keep coming here to draw water." 16Jesus said to her, "Go, call your husband, and come back." 17The woman answered him, "I have no husband." Jesus said to her, "You are right in saying, 'I have no husband'; 18for you have had five husbands, and the one you have now is not your husband. What you have said is true!" 19The woman said to him, "Sir, I see that you are a prophet. 20Our ancestors worshiped on this mountain, but you say that the place where people must worship is in Jerusalem." 21Jesus said to her, "Woman, believe me, the hour is coming when you will worship the Father neither on this mountain nor in Jerusalem. 22You worship what you do not know; we worship what we know, for salvation is from the Jews. 23But the hour is coming, and is now here, when the true worshipers will worship the Father in spirit and truth, for the Father seeks such as these to worship him. 24God is spirit, and those who worship him must worship in spirit and truth." 25The woman said to him, "I know that Messiah is coming" (who is called Christ). "When he comes, he will proclaim all things to us." 26Jesus said to her, "I am he, the one who is speaking to you."

27Just then his disciples came. They were astonished that he was speaking with a woman, but no one said, "What do you want?" or, "Why are you speaking with her?" 28Then the woman left her water jar and went back to the city. She said to the people, 29"Come and see a man who told me everything I have ever done! He cannot be the Messiah, can he?" 30They left the city and were on their way to him.

39Many Samaritans from that city believed in him because of the woman's testimony, "He told me everything I have ever done." 40So when the Samaritans came to him, they asked him to stay with them; and he stayed there two days. 41And many more believed because of his word. 42They said to the woman, "It is no longer because of what you said that we believe, for we have heard for ourselves, and we know that this is truly the Savior of the world."

Prayer: Startle us, O God, with your truth and open our hearts and our minds to your wondrous love. Speak your word to us: silence in us any voice but your own and be with us now as we turn our attention, our minds and our hearts, to you, in Jesus Christ our Lord. Amen.

YOU DON'T HAVE TO PUSH VERY HARD IN our culture to recognize that we live in a society that does not trust words very much. Words can be cheap, weasley things. You can use words to distort, to flatter, to conceal, to deceive. We don't like words, we like substance. When a politician gives a speech, what do we say? "Yeah, promises, promises." When the washing machine repair man says, "I'll be by on Thursday at 2:00, you can count on it." We don't. We didn't just start our third war last week, we are enforcing a no-fly zone. There are no civilian casualties, there is collateral damage. Words, weasley words. Give us some substance!

As Eliza Doolittle in My Fair Lady says to her two suitors, "Words, words, words. Is that all you blighters know how to do? Don't talk of stars burning above, if you're in love, show me!"

Our distrust of words is nothing new. In fact, it is as old as time. Things were going well in the Garden of Eden until there was a suspicion raised about the veracity of words. The serpent raised the possibility that words may not be all that they seem. Did God say you will die? Did God say you will not die? Whatever else we lost in the Garden — our innocence, our virtue — whatever else we lost in the Garden, we lost our language.

God gave us words to build relationships of love, to build communities of trust and righteousness. And after the Garden, men and women became liars. "Where is your brother" "I can't recall at this point in time." "Where is your sister?" "I do not know. Am I my sister's keeper?"

We are certainly proud of the kind of programs we have here at Idlewild…going out into the community and tutoring and feeding the homeless and playing baseball for inner city kids and providing resources for those down and out and supporting MIFA and the

Church Health Center and providing clean water in Ghana and Mexico and showing children from Burundi and Mexico and Binghamton how to grow a garden. That's substance! That's what I brag about to folks out there!

But more and more, I have become convinced that in large measure, the ministry that Idlewild does, is a ministry of words. It's important for us to realize that; that to be redeemed in Jesus Christ is to get our language back. The possibility of using words in ways that are full of grace and truth; words that point to justice. Just words. And I think that might be part of the story we read just a little while ago about Jesus and the woman at the well.

I mean, when you ask yourself, "what did Jesus do for that woman?" He did not heal her of any disease. He did not raise her child from the dead. He did not walk on water and dazzle her into faith. I mean, when you get right down to it, all Jesus did for that woman was talk to her. Words. Just words.

But the words He used were so unlike all the other words she had heard. They transformed her. Words of grace and truth. Now look, it is important, I think, to note that this story does not begin with words. In fact, quite to the contrary, it begins in silence.

But there is a little detail, a little surprising nuance with multiple meanings that sets the stage. You might not have even noticed it when I read it. I didn't for about 20 years. "He had to go through Samaria." Well, if you have one of those beautifully colored maps in the back of your bible, you'll see that Jesus is in Judea, and that he doesn't have to go through Samaria to get to Galilee. It seemed to be the most direct route, but Jews didn't go through Samaria — too many centuries of alienation and hostility, too much animosity, too many unclean people. But John tells us he had to go. I wonder why.

82

And the story then begins in silence. Jesus has come to the old landmark, Jacob's well; and he is resting there. A Samaritan woman comes from the town to draw water at the well. And there is silence — not a tranquil, peaceful silence, not a gentle silence — but a hard, cold, stony silence because she who came to the well was a woman. He who rested at the well was a man. She who came to the well was a Samaritan; he who rested at the well was a Jew. And between Samaritan women and Jewish men there was a wall of silence — built brick by brick, through racial and religious and sexual prejudice through the generations. Hatred and fear, through which no word was allowed to pass. "Would you give me a drink of water?" said the Jewish man to the Samaritan woman, and the wall came tumbling down. One phrase, one gentle word, "Would you give me a drink of water?" and the wall came tumbling down.

It is astounding to me how often the ministry of the church is a rather gentle word. Oh, occasionally there is a showdown with Caesar, to be sure; but most of the time, the ministry of the church is a gentle word laid out there, cutting against the cultural grain. Like the word spoken in 1955, that became a word of ministry to all of us—when a bus driver in Montgomery, Alabama told four people in the center of the bus they were going to have to move to the back. And one of them, a tired department store worker named Rosa Parks spoke so softly they said you could barely hear her voice above the sound of the bus motor. And all she said was "No....no." One word, and the wall came tumbling down.

Will Willimon, a Methodist bishop, tells about a parishioner he had when he was in South Carolina named Ann. Ann was a student in pharmaceutical school, and occasionally, she would come home for the weekend to visit her parents. And, when she did, she would come to church. After one such visit, that Sunday evening, Will got a telephone call from Ann's father. "Will, we received a very disturbing call from our Ann. She's gone back to school, and I needed to tell you about it. She's considering dropping out of pharmacy school." "Why is she doing that?" said Will. "I have no idea," said her father. "But she respects you very much, would you call her and talk some sense into her?"

He agreed to do it so the next morning he gave her a call. "Ann, what's this I hear? You know you've worked hard to get where you are. I can't imagine why you are doing this." "Well," she said, "it was your sermon yesterday. You said that God calls us to places of service and sacrifice. And it dawned on me that I am not in such a place. I am doing this for myself and my parents. I remembered that summer I spent in the church's literacy program with migrant farm workers. That's when I felt alive to the service of God. I think I want to give my life to that." There was a long silence on the other end of the phone. And then Will said, "Now, Ann, I was just preaching." One word, and the wall came tumbling down.

When the wall fell down between Jesus and the woman, I think it frightened her. You can tell that from the conversation. She responds with a flurry of words as if she's trying to build the wall back up. You know there is something comforting about a wall; it hems you in, but you don't have to deal with what's on the other side of it. But beneath the words of this woman, Jesus hears the woman. Beneath the harangue, He hears the human being. "Why is this that you a Jew, ask of me, a Samaritan woman, for a drink?" "If you knew who was asking, you would have been free to ask, and I would have given you living water." "Where are you going to get this water; you haven't even got a bucket — even Jacob had to have a bucket to get water out of the well!" "I'm not talking about water out of this well; I'm talking about living water."

That's when the woman said the fatal word, the word that caused her death and gave her life, "Give me this living water." "All right, go get your husband and bring him here." "I have no husband." "That's right. You've spoken the truth. You have no husband. You've had five husbands, and the man you're living with now, he's not your husband. You've said the truth." A lot of people have raised eyebrows about this part of the conversation — five husbands, she's had five husbands, the man she's living with now is not her husband, as if somehow she were a merry divorcee trading in husbands like sports cars, the Liz Taylor (may she rest in peace!) of ancient Samaria, something like that!

Women in the first century didn't have that kind of power. She has not been devouring husband after husband after husband; she has been devoured by a social system that, for whatever reason, has moved her from man to man to man and now gotten her to the place that she does not even have the dignity of marriage. She is, in her cultural context, worthless. And when Jesus says "You've had five husbands," he's not exposing her scandal; He's touching her wound with His word.

The ministry of the church is to touch the broken places with the word. Tom Long tells of a former student of his who graduated from seminary; she was called to be the pastor of a small Presbyterian church, small enough so that she set for herself the goal of visiting every member on the roll within the first six months. At the end of six months, she had done it. Visited every family on the roll except one. The session said "Don't go; they haven't been here in a couple of years. They're not coming back; it's a waste of time." She had her goal, however. And so one afternoon, she drove out to visit them.

Only the woman was at home. She poured mugs of coffee, and they sat at the kitchen table to talk. They talked about this. They talked about that. Then they talked about IT. A little over two years before she had been vacuuming in the back of the house while their young son played in the den. She hadn't checked on him for a while. She snapped off the vacuum cleaner, went into the den — he wasn't there. She followed his path across the den, through the patio door, across the patio to the swimming pool, where she found him.

At the funeral, she said "The people in the church were very kind. They said it was God's will." The young minister put her coffee cup down on the table. Should she touch it, or should she not? She touched it. "I'm sure the people at the church meant well. But they were wrong." "What do you mean?" "It isn't the will of God to take the life of children." "Well, then, who do you blame? I suppose you blame me," she said — her jaw set, her face reddening. "No, I don't blame you, that's not what I'm saying. I just don't think we ought to blame God." "Well then, explain it to me; you explain it to me!" "I can't explain it; I just know that God's heart broke when yours did."

The woman folded her arms. It was clear that the conversation was over. And when the young minister left, she was kicking herself. "Why didn't I leave it alone?" A couple of days later, however, the woman called and said, "My husband and I would like for you to come back out here. We don't know where this is going, but we have thought for two years that God was angry at us, and we now wonder if it is the other way around." With a word, she touched the wound.

When Jesus touched the wound, the woman became genuinely frightened. "I see," she said, "that you are a prophet, and I think I'd like to change the subject. Isn't it fascinating how we Samaritans worship in Mount Gerazim; you Jews worship at the temple in Jerusalem. Isn't that a fascinating distinction between Samaritans and Jews?" "Oh woman," He said, "the time is coming, and now is, when the mount and in the temple, it won't matter. What will matter to God is YOU and your worship in spirit and truth." "Me matter to God? Yeah, some day — when hell freezes over, when the Messiah comes."

That's when Jesus offered the best word of all, "I AM HE." I am He, the One whose word destroys the walls that hem you in. I am He. I am He, the One whose word touches your wound. I AM HE. I am He, the One who stands beside you giving your life. I am He. In the beginning was the Word and the Word was with God, and the Word was God, and the Word became flesh and dwelt among us full of grace and truth. I AM HE." And that woman received a Word and had a Word to speak and live.

And that woman, that worthless, no-count, outcast of a woman, became the first evangelist in the Gospel. She went into the city and told others about this man who touched her with a word … a word of grace and truth.

"I baptize you in the name of the Father, and the Son, and the Holy Spirit," we say to little Lucinda. Just words, but if we live into those words she will grow up in a community hearing words of grace and truth, knowing that she is beloved of God. Admittedly she has a head start because she has already heard those words from her parents.

But what about those who haven't heard a word that might touch a wound? Remember that sentence at the very beginning of the story? "Jesus had to go through Samaria." No he didn't. It made no sense. But there were people yearning for a word that he had to offer. He went to them.

And so a young man moves to Memphis; finds a place in mid-town. He drives by a big, concrete Gothic-styled structure on Union Avenue. "I wonder what kind of word I would hear there," he thinks to himself as he remembers the words that were directed at him in other churches ... words of judgment, words of hostility, words that led him out of the church. And he drives on by.

Think we should go to Samaria? Jesus had to. What do you think?

Amen.

Look for the Goodness

April 21, 2013
(Following the Boston Marathon Bombing)

Acts 9:36-43

36Now in Joppa there was a disciple whose name was Tabitha, which in Greek is Dorcas. She was devoted to good works and acts of charity. 37At that time she became ill and died. When they had washed her, they laid her in a room upstairs. 38Since Lydda was near Joppa, the disciples, who heard that Peter was there, sent two men to him with the request, "Please come to us without delay." 39So Peter got up and went with them; and when he arrived, they took him to the room upstairs. All the widows stood beside him, weeping and showing tunics and other clothing that Dorcas had made while she was with them. 40Peter put all of them outside, and then he knelt down and prayed. He turned to the body and said, "Tabitha, get up." Then she opened her eyes, and seeing Peter, she sat up. 41He gave her his hand and helped her up. Then calling the saints and widows, he showed her to be alive. 42This became known throughout Joppa, and many believed in the Lord. 43Meanwhile he stayed in Joppa for some time with a certain Simon, a tanner.

Prayer: Lord, through the reading and hearing of your word, help us to help those in need, and to make us sensitive to what they really need. And may the words of my mouth and the meditations of our hearts be acceptable in thy sight O Lord, our strength and our redeemer. Amen.

THE NEWS HAS BECOME ALMOST AS AMERICAN as apple pie, yet it still manages to shock and astound us. Who could possibly want to target so many innocent people enjoying one of the most feel-good traditions we have in this country, the Boston Marathon? I have a confession to make: When I first heard about it, riding out to a hospital in my car on Monday afternoon, I found it disturbing. I was saddened. But, maybe because some of us have gotten jaded or immune to such tragedies after the 1996 Olympics in Atlanta, Oklahoma City, Columbine, Aurora, Virginia Tech, Newtown… I didn't stay glued to the TV that night. I didn't even turn it on. I tried to suppress it, I guess, through staying busy. Didn't even bring it up during our staff meeting on Tuesday morning. Too much business to do, and so little time.

But that afternoon, while heading to another hospital, I heard that the first two victims were identified. An 8 year old boy. Full of life and energy. Close family, tight neighborhood who said he was as carefree as they come. And a 29 year old young woman who, ever since she was a child, would make it a point to go down to the finish line to cheer on the finishers.

And all of a sudden my defenses broke down… crashed. And it hit.

Like so many of you, I did what I often do during tragedy. I turned to the resources of faith: prayer and scripture.

The Lord is my shepherd, I shall not want…. Yea, though I walk through the valley of the shadow of death I will fear no evil. Thy rod and thy staff they comfort me.

And there were the words of Jesus himself:

I am the good shepherd. The good shepherd lays down his life for his sheep.

But there is another source that I still turn to at times like this. Mr. Rogers. Yes, Mr. Rogers of neighborhood fame. The same Mr. Rogers who was a Presbyterian minister. He died 10 years ago, but his wisdom has stayed with me. At one point, towards the end of his life, he was talking about how we might respond when there are bad things that happen. He recalled his mother saying "When bad things happen, look for the goodness around you. Look for the kind deeds. Don't simply focus on the bad. Look for the goodness."

There were a lot of bad things happening to the earliest followers of Jesus. The Roman authorities and religious leaders were getting frightened, and when people get frightened they lash out, and it was these disciples, who were growing exponentially in number, who were the scapegoats. They were starting to feel it. It was a hard time.

But there was goodness there that somebody felt ought to be told to future generations about the church in its earliest days, so that it could look back and laugh at its naiveté, and marvel at its idealism, and be inspired again by its teachers and saints.

Against the grand backdrop of the travels of Peter and Paul and their preaching and imprisonments, there is this one photo in the album over which Luke, the author, lingers. The story is that of the raising of one of the saints in Joppa, Tabitha was her name (in Greek, Dorcas), whom Peter raised from the dead.

Peter was in Lydda visiting at First Church there, had already healed Aeneas, when word came to him that Dorcas was failing. "Come to us without delay," was the message he got, so he came as quickly as he could.

When he arrived in Joppa where Dorcas lived, the scene at her house was one of despair. It seems as though Dorcas had succumbed to her illness and lay lifeless in her bed.

The wake was underway. Her friends have lovingly taken her body, washed it, and prepared it for burial, and then returned it to her bed for a viewing. The small house was overflowing with mourners, people just couldn't express enough the emptiness they felt without her. They came bearing the gestures of love for her family that their hearts wanted to express. And so the table in the dining room was jammed with plates bearing homemade banana bread and casseroles, potato salad and sliced cold cuts, brownies and a chocolate coconut cake; there were Jell-O molds and cut vegetables with dip.

Her friends, mostly widows, stood around helpless. They had brought with them their prized possessions, frocks and coats and blouses, things Dorcas had made on her sewing machine, necessities and niceties that Dorcas had provided them when their husbands died and they needed some help to get by.

One woman showed Peter the sweater that Dorcas had knitted one cold January when the evenings had a bite to them. Another kept running her fingers over the layette Dorcas had made for her youngest when she was born. Another placed at her feet of her body the afghan Dorcas had crocheted for the woman's mother so that the aging woman could put it over her lap and sit by the fire all cozy in the evening.

Every one of them seemed to have a story of how Dorcas' life had touched theirs, of some kindness rendered, some selfless act of devotion that she had offered. Dorcas, whose name means gazelle, was a tireless disciple whose devotion to others had inspired a network of welfare support and emotional undergirding. And you can see her almost darting about like a gazelle, first here and then there, looking after others, taking food, dropping by with some flowers, spending an afternoon with some elderly friend so that she might have some company, or sitting with a grieving widow telling her how lost she now felt in the midst of her loneliness.

In short, she was a simple woman who decided she could do some good in her life for people in her village who needed some help. And in her simple way of doing what was kindly and right she participated in the gift of eternal life. For it was resurrection faith that fueled her, an Easter strength that sustained her as in her own way she helped to make that little town of Joppa a bit more like the Kingdom of heaven. For surely in her caring and love for others something of heaven was made known and made manifest.

One more thing about Dorcas. Verse 36 of the passage tells us that "in Joppa there was a disciple whose name was Tabitha, which in Greek is Dorcas." And you don't get it in English, but in the original Greek you can't miss it. The word disciple in the sentence is feminine in gender. And it is the only place in the entire New Testament where the word disciple is feminine. There were other women who were disciples, but Dorcas alone among them has the distinction of that feminine gender in translation.

I don't know what to make of that, except to send that bit of exegesis to the Vatican and the Southern Baptist headquarters and a few other churches which shall remain nameless… those who say that women should not be leaders in the church because it is not "biblical." Someone forgot to tell Luke!

And — except that in a man's world as the ancient world was, in a religious tradition like ancient Judaism/Christianity which has a distinctly masculine spin to it, and in a culture in which women were second class citizens and widows especially were suspect — the life and work of Dorcas had a singularly important meaning to it that Luke did not want us to miss and so he described her as a disciple using the only feminine gender ending in the whole Bible, just so we wouldn't miss it.

It was by the body of this gazelle of Christian love that Peter knelt and prayed for the power of resurrection healing. Prayed so strongly and fervently that in fact Dorcas was raised from the dead, in the same way that Jairus' daughter and Lazarus had both been raised by Jesus.

That's not an easy thing for us moderns to understand so I'm not going to try. I'll just say that this was the first such miracle performed by any of the apostles after the resurrection of Jesus and so it is a clear sign that the power of the resurrection had been passed on to the church, and that the church itself and its apostles and disciples would be the vessels of God's continuing work among the people of God. This power would fuel and strengthen the church in the years to come. It strengthens us still.

Now that's a fact that is shot through Luke's account of the work of the Spirit in the early church. But he especially wants us to associate it with Dorcas. And why? Because of who Dorcas was and because of who she was not.

She was not a preacher, not a theologian, not a gifted or eloquent thinker or writer. She was not destined to make her mark on the church for her brave deeds and unusual insights. Women were not permitted that place in the early church. But she did something, nonetheless, that won more converts, touched more lives, influenced more people than any other had done in that little town of Joppa where she lived.

She took care of people. She made tunics and knitted Afghans and baked cookies and held hands and went and visited people and listened to folks when they told her their story, and she got her friends to help her, and she organized her own form of welfare system, and established her Little Sisters of the Poor. And it all had a human face to it, because it had her hands and her feet and her compassion.

She never wrote a book. There aren't any epistles named for her. She didn't do theology with the scribes and Pharisees. She never had the time to pen a gospel. She just got busy and did the work of the Spirit of Christ in her church and among her friends in Joppa.

And without that, the church is not much. You can have a church with perfect doctrine, where people recite creeds flawlessly from memory, where everybody knows the Lord's Prayer and all can say in unison the words to the 23rd Psalm, where the adult education classes are packed every Sunday and there is lofty preaching with good theology and sound doctrine.

But without somebody in that church to give it wings, somebody who runs around like a gazelle, and takes care of the widows and those whom nobody else has time for, who goes and prays with the discouraged and comforts those who grieve, and gets other folks to help her do the same, all the right doctrine and flawless theology in the world will scarcely have a chance. "You shall know them by their fruits," Jesus said.

Fortunately, here at Idlewild we have literally hundreds of "gazelles of Christian living" like that, most of them disciples of the feminine gender, but not all. I'm amazed at how often it is when I visit a nursing home or hospital, the patient says "Alan Cox was just here!" (I'm surprised they don't say, "Running around like a gazelle!") And

95

then there are our deacons, each one of them caregivers to very precious members who have devoted their lives to the church.

I wish that everyone could have experienced what I did on this past Tuesday as our Presbyterian Women honored Carol Jones, Mackey Johnson, and Regina Benson. The stories of how they shaped generations of women through the years by taking them under their wing, and studying the Bible with them and doing good deeds and showing them in non-glamorous, non-headline making ways what it means to be a disciple of Christ. They'll say it's not much. You might say the same. I say it is the power of the Resurrection transforming the world.

This is goodness. The world needs a kind of resurrection these days with bombings and crime and injustice and poverty and senators who can't even agree to simple background checks, not to mention a ban on assault weapons. It's easy to despair. But then along comes goodness in the form of these women and so many others through the years — including Catherine Berger last year and Nancy Thompson this year — and I see countless women who have bloomed where they have been planted and they shine where they have found light.

Friends, I have become convinced over time that our world is transformed not so much by the great lights that walk this earth, but by the lesser lights, the likes of Dorcas and you and me, who do what we can where we are and by what we do participate in something much greater than we might have imagined possible.

And when all is said and done, ours might not be a state funeral as the great and mighty have, but there may be a few mourners who hold up the threads and the cloths we have woven and give thanks for what we have done.

So are you despairing; afraid; saddened when bad things happen? Look for the goodness around you. Look for the kindness. And you know what? You don't have to look far.

Love in a Culture Stripped of Grace

May 14, 2006

I John 4:7–21

7 Beloved, let us love one another, because love is from God; everyone who loves is born of God and knows God. 8 Whoever does not love does not know God, for God is love. 9 God's love was revealed among us in this way: God sent his only Son into the world so that we might live through him. 10 In this is love, not that we loved God but that he loved us and sent his Son to be the atoning sacrifice for our sins. 11 Beloved, since God loved us so much, we also ought to love one another. 12 No one has ever seen God; if we love one another, God lives in us, and his love is perfected in us. 13 By this we know that we abide in him and he in us, because he has given us of his Spirit.

14 And we have seen and do testify that the Father has sent his Son as the Savior of the world. 15 God abides in those who confess that Jesus is the Son of God, and they abide in God. 16 So we have known and believe the love that God has for us.

God is love, and those who abide in love abide in God, and God abides in them.

17 Love has been perfected among us in this: that we may have boldness on the Day of Judgment, because as he is, so are we in this world. 18 There is no fear in love, but perfect love casts out fear; for fear has to do with punishment, and whoever fears has not reached perfection in love. 19 We love because he first loved us. 20 Those who say, "I love God," and hate their brothers or sisters, are liars; for those who do not love a brother or sister whom they have seen, cannot love

God whom they have not seen. 21 The commandment we have from him is this: those who love God must love their brothers and sisters also.

Prayer: Dear God, we hear about love, we talk about love, we preach about love, and we sing about love, we even dream about love. So startle us anew, so that our hearts and our minds might truly be open to your perfect love in Jesus Christ. Amen.

MIROSLAV VOLF, A LEADING theologian of our time, originally from Croatia, but now teaching at the Yale Divinity School, begins his newest book *Free of Charge* departing from the mere intellectual quest of theology and addresses the heart:

"The first thing I saw was a tear—a huge unforgettable tear in the big brown eye of a ten-year-old girl. Then I saw tears in her mother's eyes."

He is describing what it was like as he and his wife adopted three month old Nathaniel. In those tears of the birth mother and birth sister, there was, he said "just enough joy mixed with pain to underscore that pain's severity: their joy at seeing him…and their intense pain that it was the first time they'd seen him since he was just two days old, when they'd kissed him good-bye."

The birth mother later wrote a letter to them. "It is hard to know that you have a child in the world, far away from you," she wrote. It is hard, Volf said, because love passionately desires the presence of the beloved. Yet it was that same love that took deliberate and carefully planned steps that would lead to his absence. The letter was sent in hopes that they would read it to him when he grew up,

99

explaining that her decision to put him up for adoption was made for his own good. "I did it for you," she wrote, adding, "Someday you'll understand."

The professor reflects on this. "She loved him for his own sake, and therefore she would rather have suffered his absence if he flourished than to have enjoyed his presence if he languished; her sorrow over his avoidable languishing would overshadow her delight in his presence." When they parted, he said a smile had replaced the tears on the birth mother's face, but when he got home, with a child in one arm and an open album she made for him in the other, it was his turn to cry over the beauty and the tragedy of her love.

But the professor does not stop there. He then recounts what happened on the way to pick up this child where he got a different kind of gift. He and his wife had hardly gotten any sleep at all. They got in the car, rushed by the doughnut place to get the breakfast that they hadn't been able to have and returned to the road. There appeared a car in back of them, siren sounding and light flashing, and he was pulled over. Apparently he turned into a one way street, not realizing he was going the wrong way.

Not knowing that in the United States you are not supposed to get out of the car to address a police officer, he opened his door, took one step and said "Mr. Officer, we've just had this most wonderful news…" "Get back in your car," he barked. "May I explain…?" Again he was interrupted by the same bark. "Get back in your car, I said." Volf writes "Clad in a uniform with his eyes, those windows of the soul, hidden behind dark shades, he was all power, all law, and all business. His humanity? Locked up somewhere deep inside, underneath the shiny police belt buckle. His generosity? Hidden behind the badge of office. So within one hour he received a nasty ticket from a gruff cop and a tender child from a loving birth mother.

Now, he said that he didn't expect police officers to give out candy for traffic violations, but even in his old communist Yugoslavia you could usually talk to traffic police like human beings, and he said that this incident seemed to fit into a larger pattern of gracelessness slowly spreading like a disease throughout our culture. We live in a culture that has been largely stripped of grace.1

It would be hard to deny his conclusion, and we could spend all sorts of time and energy talking about why that is so. But John, the author of this little letter to a church that had experienced gracelessness from others, doesn't get caught up in those debates. He cuts right to the chase. "God is love," he writes, "and those who abide in love abide in God, and God abides in them." Ah, if it were only that simple. But then he addresses what it was that got in the way of that love. It was fear. They were afraid. It might have been because those who split from their church had said something mean-spirited like "If you all keep acting like this you're going to burn in hell." The kind of thing that people say, even if they don't mean it, but they've said it, and it hurts.

So the good pastor John reminded his little flock that they need not fear anything, not even death and the day of judgment, because, he says they are "perfected in love." And "perfect love casts out fear."

John lived in an entirely different culture, but he was able to hit the nail on the head when he looked at the greatest barrier to loving one another. Fear. We often think that hate is the opposite of love. Not so, says John. "Perfect love casts out fear." It doesn't take a Ph.D. in psychology to know that we are grasped by all sorts of fears. Abraham Heschel, that learned rabbi/theologian, wrote that "Fear is the anticipation and expectation of evil or pain, as contrasted with hope, which is the anticipation of good."2

What is it you fear? What pain or evil do you anticipate? We fear for our children of course, that they will be hurt by life, which is a silly fear because, of course, they will be hurt. Life hurts all of us sometime. So maybe it's just the severity of that hurt that we worry about.

We fear the future—the fear of the unknown, we call it. Will our investments go bad? Will we lose our job, will our health collapse. Will we fall off the wagon? Will we get accepted in the college of our choice, and if we do, will we make it there?

We fear for our safety. Just last Tuesday night our family was over at TCBY, having a little celebration and enjoying some ice cream cones. All of a sudden police cars went racing by, sirens sounding, lights flashing. I went looked over at the Walgreens and there were 10 police cars. Apparently there had been an attempted armed robbery. They nabbed the thief. (Apparently he didn't know you don't rob a store right next to the West Precinct police station!) They caught him, but still…we fear for our safety, and not just here in Midtown. Go out to Hacks Crossing and Winchester.3

We fear making the wrong decision…should we buy this house or another? Take this job or another? Marry this person or another? And we fear death to some extent…our old friend death, with whom we all must make some peace, and yet with whom we all rest uneasy.

Oh yes, we have fears and they are legion. But to quote that theologian Tina Turner, "What's love got to do with it? What about love casts out the fears of our lives?

Well, nothing, if you think love is what takes place on "Desperate Housewives" or "Do you want to marry a millionaire?" Nothing, if you think love is the kind of thing Tom Cruise jumps up and down on Oprah's sofa is about. If you see love as something that has to do with passion, emotion, a feeling that comes and goes, that kind of love has nothing to do with casting out our fears.

John was talking about a different kind of love, a kind of love that if we could get in tune with we would be able to love so freely, so fearlessly, (yes, fearlessly), that somehow we could surpass the usual limits of our human boundaries and find ourselves in a place that is good, secure, peaceful. It's the kind of love that the Psalmist wrote of years ago, words that we read at many a funeral when we are facing death: "God is my refuge and strength. A very help in trouble. Therefore I will not be afraid." (Psalm 46: 2-3)

And yet, we are afraid. We're only human, and our collective fears have led us to develop a culture that has been stripped of grace. John's challenge was to get the folks in that church he started to see that if you abide in God's love, there is nothing to fear, for perfect love casts out fear. God doesn't trade in fear. God's medium is love, for God is love, perfect love. And how do we get a handle on that perfect love? We all fall short, but one person did not fall short. There was the one who was perfect love incarnate. Perfect love reached out to us in the life, death, and resurrection of Jesus Christ. And when we see that, when we really understand that, we know that in whatever may happen in life God is our refuge and strength, a very present help in time of trouble, and we need not be afraid.

This is a message for all of us, because I know so many of the fears you have, and you know some of mine. But I especially want to address those of you who have wandered into this church recently for the first time. You have been away from church for a while. Maybe you, like John's little congregation, have been hurt by church. You may have some real problems with Jesus.

103

But maybe, just maybe those problems are with what the church has told you about Jesus, and not Jesus himself. I remember talking with the campus pastor who had approached me about becoming an ordained elder, even though I was 19 years old. "I really can't," I said, "I've got too many problems with Jesus." "I understand," he said. "But do you have problems with Jesus, or what people have said about Jesus." And since then the Jesus that I have come to know through scripture is perfect love. He is fearless in his ministry to transform lives and loves crippled by fear. He recognizes a connection with another, even one who is a murderous criminal. This perfect love reaches out to others even in the face of danger. It loves even as the smell of death is wafting in the air.

And I would invite you to be a part of a community of people to whom this fearless, perfect love of Jesus reaches out to. It surrounds us in the water that washes us in baptism. It fills us in the bread and wine that feeds us. It lifts us up in prayers and conversation offered for our encouragement and renewal. It heals us in the life-affirming touch of another, in the selfless act of another, in the rapt attention of another.

Become a part of this body of Christ and you will not find perfect love in the people here, but together we will crack open the fears that surround us.

Baptisms are always very poignant. Such small, innocent children, so fragile. We want to do all we can to protect them from hurt and pain and suffering. But we cannot. So we offer them something better. Webb and Clarke will be raised by good, yet imperfect parents, loved by good, yet imperfect grandparents, befriended by good, yet imperfect cousins. But perhaps just as importantly, nurtured by good, yet imperfect brothers and sisters in Christ. They will grow as we grow in our ability to love more perfectly those we claim as family and those we view as strangers.

They, and we, will be able to reach out with a fearless love in a culture that fears so much that it has been stripped of grace. But they, and we will be willing to risk that love because they, and we, are known in the perfect love of Jesus.

"I did it for you," the mother wrote her son. "Someday you'll understand." We've heard those words somewhere before, haven't we? Where was it? Oh yes. If we listened real closely, we heard him whisper those words on the cross. "I did it for you."

Perfect love. Amen.

[1] Miroslav Volf, Free of Charge: Giving and Forgiving in a Culture Stripped of Grace. Grand Rapids: Zondervan Press, 2006, pages 11-14
[2] Abraham Heschel, The Writings of Abraham Heschel, p. 53.
[3] This area in the suburbs had been hit this past week with a whole rash of robberies, including a bank in a grocery store.

Love Never Ends: Sounds Good, But Is It True?

February 14, 2010

(Valentine's Day, My First Sermon Following My Mother's Memorial Service.)

I Corinthians 13:1-13

1 If I speak in the tongues of mortals and of angels, but do not have love, I am a noisy gong or a clanging cymbal. 2 And if I have prophetic powers, and understand all mysteries and all knowledge, and if I have all faith, so as to remove mountains, but do not have love, I am nothing. 3 If I give away all my possessions, and if I hand over my body so that I may boast, but do not have love, I gain nothing. 4 Love is patient; love is kind; love is not envious or boastful or arrogant 5 or rude. It does not insist on its own way; it is not irritable or resentful; 6 it does not rejoice in wrongdoing, but rejoices in the truth. 7 It bears all things, believes all things, hopes all things, and endures all things. 8 Love never ends. But as for prophecies, they will come to an end; as for tongues, they will cease; as for knowledge, it will come to an end. 9 For we know only in part, and we prophesy only in part; 10 but when the complete comes, the partial will come to an end. 11 When I was a child, I spoke like a child, I thought like a child, I reasoned like a child; when I became an adult, I put an end to childish ways. 12 For now we see in a mirror, dimly, but then we will see face to face. Now I know only in part; then I will know fully, even as I have been fully known. 13 And now faith, hope, and love abide, these three; and the greatest of these is love.

Prayer: Startle us, O God, with your truth: open our minds to your word. Open our spirits to your presence. Open our hearts to your love, revealed and lived out by Jesus Christ. And in this time together, renew our trust in you to follow him and renew our courage to live lives of joyful faith. Amen.

THE REFORMED THEOLOGIAN KARL BARTH SAID that people come to church on the Sabbath with only one basic question in their minds: Is it true? Is the promise of God true? Is what we affirm true? The never-ending love and providence of God, the saving power of Jesus Christ, the comforting presence of the Holy Spirit, and the resurrection from the dead, the forgiveness of sins, and the communion of saints: Is it true?

Now I know that in a post-modern world we aren't even supposed to be asking questions like that. There is no such thing as a single, eternal truth, we are told. It's all relative. And you have heard me call for more uncertainty in matters of faith, believing that the certainty of fundamentalism closes off the minds that God gave us, and diminishes the unfathomable mystery of God.

But today I'd like to give my shot at an answer. It's because this is a question that has been at the forefront of my faith in a new way over the past month. And because so many of you have cared so deeply, and have responded so beautifully to my grief following the death of my mother, I wanted to share with you a bit of my own reflections in a way that I hope will be helpful to all. For you have reminded me of a lesson that I learned long ago from my mother as well as my father: love not only begets love, it transmits strength.

107

Mom had what we call a "good death." Eighty-eight years old, married to my father for over 60 years, until Thanksgiving they would still go down to the fitness center 5 days a week, and if they missed a Sunday morning at Central Presbyterian Church in Atlanta, they would get a phone call from someone just making sure everything was all right. This past Thanksgiving week-end we all met in Murray, Kentucky for a wedding in which I officiated for my nephew and his bride. Mom wasn't feeling well, but the clinic gave her some antibiotics and she made the wedding.

It was the following week that we admitted her to the hospital…fluid on the lungs we were told, and for several weeks the doctors debated if it was pneumonia or cancer or something else. Finally a laparoscopy determined that it was a very, very rare form of cancer, so rare that the oncologist, who is my age, had never seen it before. And mercifully, it was a very, very rapidly progressing form of cancer.

You remember I drove down there after church on January 3 and spent several nights with her in the hospital. She was very weak, but still had her wits about her. When I arrived there Monday morning I leaned over and kissed her and said, "Mom, it's Steve. Your favorite son." She looked at me and said "Don't go there." She and Dad have 3 sons, all preachers, so there has always been some good-natured ribbing about that. My sister was always wise enough to stay out of those debates!

But Tuesday night was one of those terrible, difficult, sleepless nights. She had this fluid but didn't have the strength to cough it up fully. So I stood there wiping her mouth, stroking her forehead and just reminding her all night of all the people that loved her, and were praying for her; all the people whose lives were made better because of her, over and over again. And of course I was thinking of all those nights in which she stayed up all night nursing four kids back to health. It was a terrible, beautiful night.

The next morning we decided to call in hospice and take her home, which is where she said she wanted to go. She came home on Thursday, in time to watch her beloved Texas Longhorns get off to a 6-0 lead in the national championship before she drifted off to sleep. (We never let her know how it ended!) The family kept vigil, some there, some around the country, until on Sunday afternoon Deedee, my sister, called us 3 brothers and we all agreed to call in at 3:30 Eastern time and sing one of her favorite hymns to her.

You see, we were always a singing family. Six of us would gather around the piano and sing hymns and old 30's and 40's favorites while my mother or Jim, my brother, would play. When we would drive to Texas each summer, we would sing. (This was before IPods, and even FM radio stations!) On Christmas mornings we would open our presents, get dressed, and head down to the hospital downtown with another family and sing carols to the patients and nurses who were there on Christmas morning.

So at the anointed time, 6 or 7 people gathered around her bed with two cell phones and a computer which had "skyped" David and his wife Ann Marie from Murray, and we all sang her father's favorite hymn:

> "Open my eyes that I may see, glimpses of truth thou hast for me
> Place in my hands the wonderful key that shall unclasp and set me free.
> Silently now I wait for Thee, ready my God, Thy will to see
> Open my eyes, illumine me, Spirit Divine."

It was then and only then, that that evening my father could go into her room and sit by her side, holding her hand and say, "Margaret, I've always loved you and always will. It's OK to let go, because we'll see each other soon." She whispered "I love you."

The next morning the three boys all called in and said the same thing to her over the phone. I reminded her what we Presbyterians always said. (You have to know this about mom. She was sinfully proud to be Presbyterian. She loved people from all traditions and faiths, but it still mystified her that, if people had a choice, why people would choose not to be a Presbyterians!). I told her "Mom, in life and in death we belong to God. So we're going to be OK, and you're going to be OK, because we all belong to God. I love you." Her final words were "I love you."

She died about an hour later. It was a good death. What made it good? Well, it wasn't because she had worked her way through Elizabeth Kubler Ross's stairway of emotional and ethical development in dying, which, as Tom Long points out in a recent book on funerals, is a fiction of therapeutic culture. He makes the point that people die pretty much as they have lived. If someone has been enraged throughout life, we can expect rage at the end. A person who tried to bargain with life, family, physicians, and God on death's door has probably tried to cut a few deals before. But a person who blessed the world at death has not learned this in the last few hours of life, but has been shaped to live a life of blessing. (Case in point: Jim Gibb Johnson!)   So Tom concludes: The best preparation for dying a [good] Christian death, then, is living a [good] Christian life."

And that journey begins at baptism. Baptism is about dying and rising with Christ. Baptism is about being washed clean from sin. Baptism is about being welcomed into a community of faith as a brother or sister in Christ. Baptism is about responding to a holy call and setting out on an adventure of faith.

It is obvious that my mother's parents and her community of faith took those vows seriously. After graduating from the University of Texas she studied at the Presbyterian School of Christian Education in Richmond and became a Christian educator. She and dad married and raised four children in a community of faith and later worked there at PSCE nurturing future leaders of the church. And when we moved to Atlanta, she became the Director of Refugee Resettlement for our denomination.

Now what was remarkable about this position is that for mom, it was not just a job. She was not just an administrator overseeing the program, or just a church bureaucrat shuffling papers, out of touch with the local church. No, this was a calling, a response to her baptism. She traveled to refugee camps around the world and saw the suffering of Vietnamese in Malaysia, or Palestinians in Jordan, or Nigerians in Benin. And because of those experiences, she went back to scripture that she had learned as a child and studied in graduate school, with new eyes. Matthew 25: 31-46, the parable of sheep and goats in which Jesus reminds his listeners that those who feed the hungry and minister to the "least of these" are ministering to Jesus himself became her roadmap for her Christian life.

I was able to hear her speak on the floor of presbyteries and in churches, (she helped several churches I served re-settle refugees,) and she would always tell that story of "the least of these." One time when she was trying to encourage a church to open its doors to a family fleeing persecution she spoke and then took questions. Toward the end a man in the back stood up and said, "This is all well and good, but it costs money. How are we supposed to pay for it?" And mom responded simply, "Matthew 25."

I had the opportunity several weeks ago to go over to Temple Israel to hear Rabbi Jeffrey Salkin. He reminded us that in the book of Leviticus, with all those laws, that we are commanded to love God one time. We are commanded to love our neighbor one time. But we are commanded to love the stranger, the alien, the sojourner, no less than 36 times. I hadn't realized that, but I think my mother could have told us that. She and my father practiced a life of radical hospitality.

So much so that I never knew who I would be sharing a room with when I came home. It started, I suppose when the 4 children were all young and my cousin's high school was shut down in Virginia due to massive resistance to desegregation orders. So he came and lived with us for a year. Then my cousins moved to the Dominican Republic to start the Peace Corps there, and there was no school for Peggy, another cousin, so she came and lived with us. And then we had a foreign exchange student from Austria live with us for a year.

That started the Montgomery hospitality suites. One time I came home from seminary and walked in the door only to find a Vietnamese family staying with us. They had to flee their refugee camp quickly, and landed in Los Angeles without a place to stay, so they stayed with us until a church in Minnesota took them in. One time I came home and there was a refugee from Russia. He stayed for a year. There was Carlos from Honduras, who lived with mom and dad when the Atlanta Braves won the World Series. Mom's enthusiasm for the Braves was contagious, and he caught pennant fever! There was the Nicolas family from Sri Lanka, who were targeted because they had a mixed marriage. She was Sinhalese and he was Tamil. They contacted the Presbyterian Church, and mom not only found her a job the second day she arrived in America, and helped him complete his education and restart his career as an

112

engineer, but was pretty much solely responsible for them being granted asylum in this country. And then there was the time one of my friends from seminary let me know he had been admitted to Emory Medical School in his quest to be a minister and a doctor. "If you need a place to stay for a few weeks, why don't you call my parents?" Scott Morris ended up living with them 4 years.

So do you see why I am so messed up? And so passionate about radical hospitality? The mandate from Jesus himself to care for the least of these, our brothers and sisters?

All of which is to say that mom lived with a vision in which her family was larger than her family; and she learned that in the church, where she believed until her dying day that the church ought to be the one place where no one feels excluded, all feel vital, where healing happens and where reconciliation occurs. She knew the church well, and knew its shortcomings perhaps better than anyone here, but she never gave up on the church because at the heart of her faith, she knew God never gave up on her.

So what have been some of my learnings through this? Here are just a few:

> "Blessed are those who mourn, for they shall be comforted."

I have discovered that this promise of God is true. One would think that after an incredibly faithful life of 88 years, 4 children (3 of whom are preachers, one who is an educator), 11 grandchildren and 3 great-grandchildren; not to mention over 60 years of marriage, a life-time of Christian service, that I wouldn't have feelings of grief. And though the joy is greater than the sorrow, the sorrow is still there. As I've said before, the sadness is for me and not for her, but I was surprised that, even though in those final weeks we were hoping for a swift and painless death, when it came, I felt it. I've learned that you can prepare for it, but you really can't prepare for it.

I received an email from a friend who reminded me that normal is a cycle on a washing machine, and there is no normal way to grieve. We all have to find our own way. All four of us children handled it somewhat differently. For one, the tears never came, for another, the tears flowed more freely.

But in the midst of grief, there was so much comfort. Much of it was provided by you. I never knew I could be surrounded by so many prayers, receive so many cards or expressions of love. They will be with me till my dying day, I assure you. And I am going to ask that you continue to remember especially my father, as his daily life will change the most. He has resumed his work-out routine at the fitness center and hasn't missed a Sunday at church. His church has been the church for him and just last Sunday he went to watch the Super Bowl at a church gathering. But I cherish your ongoing prayers for him, and for my sister Deedee as the one who lives there in Atlanta, and for whom most of the burdens have fallen upon.

But the greater comfort of course, is found in another learning:

"In life and in death, we belong to God."

This promise of God, which is on virtually every page of scripture, is true. I can't prove it like a mathematician would prove the Pythagorean theory. But I know it to be true. We do not know what life is like after death, we only know that the life the deceased have is in God. And so the one conviction that I can state unequivocally is that death does not have the final word. The God we know in Jesus Christ, speaks the last word.

I have a friend who, when his mother died, people would come up saying "I'm sorry you lost your mother." And he would reply, "Oh, we haven't lost her. We know where she is." I would add, "We know who she is with." For like Paul, I am convinced, no, convicted, that there is nothing that will ever separate mom or any of us from the love of God in Christ Jesus. It is true.

> "Do not neglect to show hospitality to strangers, for by doing so some have entertained angels unaware."

This promise of God is true. I've met a few of the angels mom and dad entertained myself. After all, what do angels do in the Bible? They bless us, and I was surely blessed again and again. And they tell us not to fear. And hearing their stories and all that they had overcome, reminded me that we ultimately have nothing to fear, for we are in the hands of God.

But this isn't just a call for us to open our homes to refugees—not everyone can do that, (though this certainly does have implications for our nation's immigration policy!), but because this is true, it is a challenge for all of us in this beloved community we call the church to show radical hospitality to strangers. I would love to see you jumping over pews to make sure that when people enter this sanctuary that you do not know, they will feel welcome, that no one will feel ignored or forgotten or anything less than loved by God. Or I'd love to see you just sitting down and eating with and talking with some of our friends from the streets on Thursday evenings at More Than a Meal. You just might be entertaining angels unaware.

Gary Charles reminded us at the funeral that we do this not because people are always so loveable, but because God conceived us in love

115

and gives us all the faith we need to live in that love. Which brings us to a final learning:

"Love never ends."

Hear me now: This is true. This is true. Though mom has died, her life and her love will go on bearing new fruit. Her spirit will keep on descending upon those of us who knew her.

Theologian Elizabeth Johnson wrote that when the church affirms its belief in the communion of the saints, it means to say that death's destructive power cannot sever the bonds holding persons in communion, for these bonds are grace, love, and community of God's own being. In dying," she concludes, "one falls into the living God and is quickened by loving-kindness which is forever faithful."

With your help, may we continually remind each other of our baptism, and may we together seek consolation in that love which never ends, and find peace in the dazzling grace that always is.

Oh, and there is one more thing…

I love you.

Amen.

Memorial Day

May 29, 2010
(Memorial Day Weekend)

John 15:12–17

12 "This is my commandment, that you love one another as I have loved you. 13 No one has greater love than this, to lay down one's life for one's friends. 14 You are my friends if you do what I command you. 15 I do not call you servants any longer, because the servant does not know what the master is doing; but I have called you friends, because I have made known to you everything that I have heard from my Father. 16 You did not choose me but I chose you. And I appointed you to go and bear fruit, fruit that will last, so that the Father will give you whatever you ask him in my name. 17 I am giving you these commands so that you may love one another.

Prayer: Come, O God, into the quiet of this holiday week-end. In the midst of leisure, may we remember men and women who served their country and died. May we remember, as well, your dream of harmony and peace for your creation. And may we remember your promise to dwell among us and be our God. In Jesus Christ our Lord, Amen.

O N MEMORIAL DAY, OF ALL DAYS, IT IS IMPORTANT to remember. But it is easy to let the memory fade.

Frank Buckles hopes the memory does not fade. Do you know that name? This past February he turned 109, and he is the sole remaining American veteran to have served in World War I, often called the Great War. He is the honorary chairperson of a committee to have a monument erected in Washington to honor those who paid the ultimate price of their lives in that war. That war is fading from our memory, says Douglas Martin, a New York Times writer several years ago. He writes:

World War I was so vile that nobody ever expected to see anything like it ever again. The lads who marched into fire bombs, mud and poisonous gas, would never be forgotten. Or would they? In tens of thousands of parks, traffic triangles, and cemeteries in every corner of America, World War I memorials are crumbling faster than they can be shored up by people who consider them sacred, even as the events they mourn, praise and implicitly question, fade deeper into the mist.

And then Mr. Martin editorialized:

The Great War solved nothing, proving only that human beings, acting in organized fashion, could kill one another, more efficiently than ever dreamed. Most of the American dead were buried near the fields of battle. So their friends and families built shrines near the fields where they hit baseballs and held the hands of pretty girls. These tributes … were meant to be eternal.

But the monuments are deteriorating. 116,500 Americans died in the First World War. There were 4.3 million in uniform. One remains.

I will never forget my first visit to the Vietnam Memorial in Washington. This was the war that was closest to me and my generation. I went there and looked in the books and found the names of those I knew etched in the black granite wall. There he was—Joe Monaham, who was on the track team with me. Even though he was a senior and I was a freshman, I remember him speaking to me and treating me kindly. He was engaged to be married to a girl in our church. There was Jon Smith. Sat next to him in English class, along with his twin brother Chris. Identical as any two twins could be. Never could tell them apart. Both names were up there.

It is important to remember.

Tom Are is the pastor of the Village Presbyterian Church in Kansas City. He tells of one of the members, a woman named Dusty, who heard that her pastor was going to Washington and intended to visit the Vietnam Memorial. So she cornered him after worship one Sunday. She said "Tom, somebody was in Washington a while ago and came home and told me that she could not find my son's name on the wall. She said 'His name isn't on the wall.' Tom, will you look for him?" Tom promised that he would. He and his family walked the wall a few weeks later. They all searched and searched and found the boy's name. No one in this world was happier than Dusty when Tom was able to report to her that her son's name was indeed there. He was remembered.

If peace is important—if peace is the highest priority on God's agenda—and there is no way to argue that it isn't, then memory of war, the waste, the suffering, the millions and millions of combatants and innocent civilians who have died; the unleashing of the very worst of our humanity: pogroms, massacres, holocaust, genocide—that's all a part of the memory. But so is the heroism, the self-sacrifice, the nobility, the laying down of one's life, the highest and best of our humanity.

We must remember it all, but it is easy to forget. And when we forget those who fought and died, we forget the ideals that they fought for, and our memories become very selective. We forget that truth is always the first casualty of war. We forget that our motives have not always been pure in going to war. We forget the true costs of war, such as the moral wounds of war. The Rand Corporation recently estimated that 300,000 veterans are currently suffering from post-traumatic stress syndrome. One quarter of a million veterans of wars since Vietnam are serving time behind bars. And we forget our nation's highest and best principles, which come from the Judeo-Christian tradition, of the God-given dignity and rights and liberty of every man and woman in creation.

It is also important to remember that war and violence begins in the mind, and though our forebears fought and died for free speech, even, as one person recently suggested, the free speech of idiots, the kind of angry rhetoric that has been displayed on the air waves and at rallies, and even within the halls of Congress do a disservice to our very best ideals. When a talk show host says "We have to get rid of these people"—and calls them a name unsuitable for a pulpit, he crosses a line between expressing political preferences and inciting violence. When some of our political leaders shout "You lie!" to the President, or "baby-killer" to a strong pro-choice Congressman, then sure enough, violent and potentially violent acts begin to happen, and it is not difficult to see the connection between the rhetoric of rage and violent behavior.

Our fragile experiment in republican democracy, which is based upon the God-given liberty of every individual for which hundreds of thousands have died, leans heavily upon the tradition of civil dialogue—and that tradition fades in the midst of shouts and threats of violence, and soon we find that, according to the Southern Poverty Law Center, violent, "nativist extremist groups have increased 80% since President Obama took office." And soon you have an unhinged believer flying his Cessna into an IRS building in

Texas, or a father and a son ready to take down any officers that get in their way in West Memphis.

When we remember faithfully, you see, we can't help but weep—to remember and give thanks for those who laid down their lives for us, to mourn for those we've loved and lost in the prime of life; to grieve for every parent's child who has died on all sides of conflicts. It is then that perhaps our voices might be lowered and we can restore our civic, and civil, discourse.

So we remember, but we must not simply remember those who have gone before us. We also remember those who serve in the armed forces today in terribly harsh conditions, those who go back for three, four or five tours of duty, those who are suffering and dying. This weekend the toll in Afghanistan reached 1,000 casualties. Iraq is over 4,500. We also remember those who are increasingly pawns in a global game of pride and power, innocents who are every bit as precious in God's eyes as our own children. (Has there ever been a more disrespectful and impersonal term used to describe innocent civilians killed as "collateral damage?")

This is the challenge for many of us, for feelings and convictions about the wars we are currently fighting in Iraq and Afghanistan are diverse and deep. People of good faith, starting at the same place— the security and safety of the nation and the peace of the world— come to diametrically opposite conclusions about what we are doing and how we are doing it, whether we should have invaded Iraq in the first place, whether and when we should leave both countries, and how. And, as is always the case, preachers on both sides invoke the name of God, God's justice and God's righteousness, to support their point of view.

Abraham Lincoln pondered this irony in the midst of the Civil War. North and South read the same bible, he said, pray to the same God, yet God did not answer the prayer of either side fully.

And I am one who has had, and has expressed deep concerns about these wars. But then I remember Father Barkemeyer, a Roman Catholic priest from Chicago. From the start he shared with his congregation reservations and misgivings about what we are doing in Iraq, but he serves as an Army chaplain there. He said "This is not the place I would choose to be, but I'm supposed to be here. This is all about taking care of sons and daughters, not about the justice of the cause." And so he travels through the dangerous streets of Ramadi by Humvee, to say mass and to visit lonely and frightened young Americans. He administers last rites to dozens of victims of car bombs and roadside bombs, prays with the wounded and dying in the military emergency room, and is available at all hours of the day and night to talk with soldiers troubled by fear and religious uncertainty.

And, oh yes, in his quarters, Father Barkemeyer keeps a supply of children's books and a video camera so parents can read bedtime stories to their children 6,000 miles away.

God bless Father Barkemeyer. God bless those young parents. God bless their children. God bless them all.

"No one has great love than this, to lay down one's life for one's friends."

Jesus was saying goodbye to his disciples in that upper room. Later he would be betrayed, arrested, tortured and the crowds' rage won the day as he was executed.

But this evening he summed it all up:

"Do not let your hearts be troubled. Believe in God, believe also in me."

"In my Father's house there are many dwelling places."

"I will not leave you orphaned, I am coming to you."

"I am the vine, you are the branches."

"I have said these things to you so that my joy may be in you and that your joy may be complete."

But right in the middle, there is there is the most memorable summation:

"This is my commandment, that you love one another as I have loved you. No one has greater love than this, to lay down one's life for one's friends."

As he faced his own death, what Jesus wanted his friends to know and remember was that the whole creation is full of God's love; that he, himself—his life, his teaching, his death—was an expression, a picture of God's love; that this human race, with all its amazing diversity, is the expression of God's love; that all the religious traditions and rituals and theologies and institutions in the world are for the purpose of acknowledging, saying thank you for and pouring that love of God back into the life of the world.

And one more thing, one very personal thing: If you want to live your life fully, every year of it, every week and day and minute of it, you have to lay it down, give it away. You have to find someone or something you love so much that you are willing to live for it, or die for it. This is the Christian secret. To live the very best life you possibly can, you have to give it away—to a child, a beloved, your friends, your faith, your church, or the great ideas and principles of our nation.

So may we remember them all this day with deep gratitude, but also with confession, as we confess our tendency to be more willing to kill than to lay down our lives; more willing to glorify war than to understand the things that make for peace; more willing to cause suffering than to suffer; more willing to take up our weapons than our crosses.

And may we remember the one who taught us and continues to teach us, the one who said "No one has greater love than this, to lay down one's life for one's friends," and pray that he might teach us to beat our swords into plowshares and spears into pruning hooks. It is then that we could join in singing that old spiritual, "Ain't gonna study war no more."

That would truly honor those we remember.

Amen.

Nuthin' Much To Look At

June 17, 2012

I Samuel 16:1-13

The Lord said to Samuel, "How long will you grieve over Saul? I have rejected him from being king over Israel. Fill your horn with oil and set out; I will send you to Jesse the Bethlehemite, for I have provided for myself a king among his sons." 2Samuel said, "How can I go? If Saul hears of it, he will kill me." And the Lord said, "Take a heifer with you, and say, 'I have come to sacrifice to the Lord.' 3Invite Jesse to the sacrifice, and I will show you what you shall do; and you shall anoint for me the one whom I name to you." 4Samuel did what the Lord commanded, and came to Bethlehem. The elders of the city came to meet him trembling, and said, "Do you come peaceably?" 5He said, "Peaceably; I have come to sacrifice to the Lord; sanctify yourselves and come with me to the sacrifice." And he sanctified Jesse and his sons and invited them to the sacrifice.

6When they came, he looked on Eliab and thought, "Surely the Lord's anointed is now before the Lord." 7But the Lord said to Samuel, "Do not look on his appearance or on the height of his stature, because I have rejected him; for the Lord does not see as mortals see; they look on the outward appearance, but the Lord looks on the heart." 8Then Jesse called Abinadab, and made him pass before Samuel. He said, "Neither has the Lord chosen this one." 9Then Jesse made Shammah pass by. And he said, "Neither has the Lord chosen this one." 10Jesse made seven of his sons pass before Samuel, and Samuel said to Jesse, "The Lord has not chosen any of these." 11Samuel said to Jesse, "Are all your sons here?" And he said, "There remains yet the youngest, but he is keeping the sheep." And Samuel said to Jesse, "Send and bring him; for we will not sit down until he comes here." 12He sent and brought him in. Now he was ruddy, and had beautiful eyes, and was handsome. The Lord said, "Rise and anoint him;

for this is the one." 13Then Samuel took the horn of oil, and anointed him in the presence of his brothers; and the spirit of the Lord came mightily upon David from that day forward. Samuel then set out and went to Ramah.

Prayer: As we gather to hear your word, O God, may we find comfort where we need solace, discomfort where we need to be shaken from our lethargy, and a startled amazement at the ways you work through history, and in our lives. And now may the words of my mouth and the meditations of our hearts be acceptable in thy sight, O Lord, our strength and our redeemer. Amen.

HE WAS NUTHIN' MUCH TO LOOK AT. Nuthin' much at all. Oh, there had been a time when he was every inch a king. When God's prophet Samuel found him, he was something to look at, really something! Listen to the way he was described: "There was not a man among the people of Israel more handsome than Saul; from his shoulders upward he was taller than any of the people." (Sam. 9:2) Head and shoulders above everybody else....both literally and figuratively.

But it did not last. It turned sour. As a king, Saul bombed out. And now, he was nuthin' much to look at. And Samuel, who had talked him into being a king, now had to tell him he was through.

Saul was alone, rejected, isolated, and torn. He was nuthin' much to look at. Nuthin' much at all.

And so Samuel sets out again to find a king. Samuel is a man in the middle. He stands for the old ways and traditions, but he is involved in the transition to new ways. He had reached retirement age, and he wanted to turn thing over to his sons, but "there were a bunch of crooks who sold justice to the highest bidder." (Buechner, *Peculiar Treasures*, P. 151.)

Samuel really does not have very much motivation or enthusiasm for what he is doing. The things and qualities he had fought for— change, a progressive understand of Yahweh—he now fought against. He had become tired, a nitpicker, and out of step with those around him. He, too, was beginning to be nothing much to look at. Nothing much at all.

So, reluctantly, he sets about his task of finding a new king. And he thinks he has found him. Eliab by name. The eldest and tallest of the sons of Jesse, a man who lives in Bethlehem. Maybe everything would be all right. Samuel looked at Eliab and said to himself, "Surely the Lord' anointed is before me, ah, that is, before the Lord. But—and deep down you know this was going to happen—the Lord said to Samuel, "Beauty is only skin deep, Samuel. Don't fall for appearance again as you did with Saul. You might think Eliab looks like a king, but I am looking at the inward person. And I do not see a king there, not in his heart."

Samuel knew right then he was in trouble. This whole thing was getting out of hand. Samuel had each of the sons of Jesse parade before him, flex their muscles, swing their swords, do whatever you have kings-to-be do. And with each one, he wondered if this one was to be the new king. But each time, Yahweh said, "Nope! Not that one! And each time they got smaller and younger, less kingly in appearance. And then there were none.

Samuel was almost afraid to ask the question. He was afraid of the answer he knew he would get. "Oh, by the way, Jesse, you don't have any other sons, do you? I mean, you don't have any more than these seven sons?"

Jesse did. He had one more. "There is one, but he's out watching the sheep. And he's the youngest." And Samuel said, "Well, fetch him; for we can't eat supper until he gets here anyway!"

And there he is. The new king. A mere shepherd boy. The runt of the family. The caboose. He is nothing much to look at. Nuthin' much.

I have a friend who has the most expressive and articular sigh that I have ever heard. It can express total joy or utter exasperation. I can hear Samuel sigh like that as he looks at David and realizes that this new boy is the new king. S I G H H H H H. You need a commanding presence in a king. But here he is….this runt of a boy, this teen-ager with pimples on his cheeks.

Oh, there's really nothing wrong with him. He's just not much…he's little, he's young, inexperienced, a teen-ager. He's just…nothin' much to look at!

It's funny how God works. You've heard the expression: "How odd of God to choose the Jews." But just think of the Jews that God choose to choose. How often is it that God seems to have a definite bias for the young, the small, and the least, the apparently insignificant? When Saul was named king, he came from the smallest tribe. And now here is David, the youngest and smallest member of the family. And there was Abel over Cain, Rachel over Leah, Joseph over all the older brothers, the prodigal son over the elder brother, Bethlehem over Jerusalem.

It must be God's way of reminding us that God is in control of human destiny, that what happens is at God's beck and call and not ours; that history is, after all, God's story and not ours. And our task is to try to align our lives, our actions, our values with God's purposes.

But Samuel is still thinking of the press release. And as he looks at the shepherd boy he says, "Sigh. Well, he is ruddy and he does have nice eyes." And Yahweh says, "Arise, anoint this boy with pretty eyes, for this is he."

He was nuthin' much to look at. Nuthin' much at all. But God chose him. God chose him to change history. For out of the mess and chaos of their history, God was making another new beginning. God was in charge, in control, using the events and personalities behind the events, flawed through they were, to order the destiny of humanity after God's purpose and will.

Isn't that what the history of the Bible, and indeed, our own faith history is all about, anyway? God moving through our own fallibilities and our mistakes and our imperfect processes; giving us another chance after chance after chance, offering us a new beginning? In Saul, in this shepherd boy, David, in our own history. And won't you believe it? In you, in me, in us!

God is always looking for opportunities for newness. And sometimes God's purposes are accomplished because of our best efforts, and sometimes they are accomplished in spite of our best efforts. Samuel wanted to see the very best that Jesse had to offer, but Samuel ended up being surprised, for God worked through the very least in order to bring newness into the world.

Today, our very faith is at stake. In the midst of a culture that is increasingly despairing, lonely, hiding behind the internet which was supposed to bring us closer together; a society increasingly consumed with materialism and consumerism; a nation that has virtually abandoned the concept of "the common good" and yielded to a crass individualism, we must think the new. I know that much of the mainstream culture thinks that we in the mainstream churches have little to offer, but Idlewild is thriving because we have always pushed forward, and we are going to continue to push forward, trying as best we can to be a faithful witness to the Gospel, making the outrageous claim that a certain Jesus Christ has shown us a better way, opening up ourselves to the possibility that God can use us in ways that we haven't even imagined yet....use us, fallible, imperfect people...for God's purposes and will.

Michael Lindvall is a Presbyterian Pastor in New York City who writes of the mythical town of North Haven, Minnesota and the pastor of the Presbyterian Church there named David. David and his wife Annie had served this little church for four years and upon coming home from a vacation he was reflecting upon how good it was to be coming home. It took four years, but it really felt like home now. As soon as they got home they found a note from the church secretary on the porch door. "Minnie McDowell is pretty sick; thinks she's dying again, better get over there soon."

This had happened on several different occasions. Minnie knew exactly how she was supposed to die: at home, in bed, in a fresh nightgown, with the pastor present. But as the doctor explained, "The only problem with Minnie's plans is that she's not sick."

So anyway the good pastor popped in the car and went over to Minnie's house, where her husband, Angus, answered the door and took him up to Minnie's room. He sat down, and Minnie said, "Ask me the question, pastor."

Lindvall writes: "The question, I had come to know on my last two visits to Minnie's deathbed, was an essential part of her very precise plans for the day. The pastor was to ask "Are you prepared to die?" The die-ee was to answer, "Yes, pastor, I am." Then the pastor read the 23rd Psalm and prayed briefly, concluding with the Lord's Prayer. Then the die-ee was to die. That was how it was properly done. We had done it twice before, except the last part."

And so Pastor Dave smiled pastorally at Minnie and said, "Are you prepared to die?"

He writes: "I almost slid off my chair when she said, "No." Her lower lip started to quiver and she looked away from me at the wall. I squeezed her hand as Angus patted me on the back and said, "Minnie's got something she's got to get off her chest." At which Minnie choked out the words: "No, Angus, you tell him."

"David," Angus began, "you'll remember that I was the chairman of the Pastor Nominating Committee that called you to be our pastor 4 years ago. We received 28 dossiers from ministers. We read them all and narrowed the choice down to two, you and the Reverend Mr. Hardwick Benson of Indianapolis. We invited both you and Mr. Benson to visit North Haven. We listened to the both of you preach up in Willmar."

David remembered it fondly. What elation, he thought. What affirmation, when a simple handwritten note came four days later postmarked "N. Haven, Minn." There was no heading, only a date, and then, "Dear Sir, We are most pleased to inform you…"

"David," Angus went on as his eyes sited from me to his wife, "Minne was the secretary to our committee. She typed up the letters. She typed one to the Reverend Benson and one to you. Somehow they got in the wrong envelops. Mr. Benson got your letter and you got Mr. Benson's letter."

At this, Minnie started dabbing her eyes with her hanky and then wrapping it tightly around her index finger in a sort of penitential self- mortification. "We never realized the mistake until you called on the phone to say yes, you'd come. You were so eager, we just decided, well, what the heck, and let it go. I just couldn't die with such a thing in my conscience."

Lindvall writes: "All of a sudden, it wasn't Minnie who was dying. It was me. Noting my stunned silence, she pushed herself up to a sitting position, ordered Angus to make hot tea, and resolved to postpone her death. Angus commented on how amazingly helpful my visit was to her, saying "A person always feels better when they get something off their chest." There may have been unburdened, but mine was loaded." I got back in the car and headed home, wherever that was."

Well, the good pastor goes on to realize that this was home, that the will of God is an intricate weaving of incidents and accidents, plans and providence. Sometimes it works through us, sometimes in spite of us, but in all things, it can work for good.

God is in control. God can take broken, fragmented, imperfect people, often the smallest and weakest (by the ways of the world) and change history.

That includes you. That includes me. That includes us…together.

Patriotism Is Not Enough

February 10, 2002
(As Our Nation was Preparing to Invade Iraq)

Isaiah 43:18-25

18Do not remember the former things, or consider the things of old. 19I am about to do a new thing; now it springs forth, do you not perceive it? I will make a way in the wilderness and rivers in the desert. 20The wild animals will honor me, the jackals and the ostriches; for I give water in the wilderness, rivers in the desert, to give drink to my chosen people, 21the people whom I formed for myself so that they might declare my praise.

22Yet you did not call upon me, O Jacob; but you have been weary of me, O Israel! 23You have not brought me your sheep for burnt offerings, or honored me with your sacrifices. I have not burdened you with offerings, or wearied you with frankincense. 24You have not bought me sweet cane with money, or satisfied me with the fat of your sacrifices. But you have burdened me with your sins; you have wearied me with your iniquities. 25I, I am He who blots out your transgressions for my own sake, and I will not remember your sins.

Prayer: Almighty God, from whom all thoughts of truth and peace proceed, kindle, we pray Thee, in the hearts of all people the true love of peace; and guide with Thy pure and peaceable wisdom those who take counsel for the nations of the earth; that in tranquility Thy kingdom may go forward till the earth be filled with the knowledge of Thy love. This we pray through Jesus Christ our Lord. Amen.

-Francis Paget, 1851-1911

133

IN THE EARLY MORNING HOURS OF October 12, 1915, Nurse Edith Cavell was tied to the stake in German-occupied Belgium and shot as a traitor. Long before that "war to end all wars"-World War I—she had for many years headed a nursing home in Belgium, and even after war had broken out she had remained at her post, where, together with her nurses, she gave care to injured soldiers regardless of nationality, whether German, French, or English. Miss Cavell was arrested as a traitor by the Germans for the "crime" of assisting soldiers in their flight to neutral Holland. Determined to make an example of her, the Germans tried her under military law, under a military tribunal, and without adequate counsel she was presumed guilty, found so, and sentenced to death and executed within ten hours of the judgement. The whole episode was shrouded in vindictive haste and stealth, and through the years she has been regarded as one of the few true heroines of World War I.

Her last moments, and her final words, are described as follows by an eyewitness:

"After receiving the sacrament, and within minutes of being led out to her death, she said, 'Standing as I do in view of God and eternity, I realize that patriotism is not enough. I must have no hatred or bitterness toward anyone."

On the base of her statue in London are carved the words: "Patriotism is not enough."

I have thought about that sentiment a great deal in the past few weeks and months. Edith Cavell was a great Christian, the daughter of an Anglican priest, and it would be easy for us to dismiss those words as brave but too simple; as eloquent but enigmatic, as true in her day, but irrelevant in this day.

And yet, I have struggled mightily with the tension between my love of country and my love of God; my desire to be a conscientious citizen and my desire to be a faithful Christian; to support my president whenever I can, and to be obedient to my Lord at all times.

Sometimes there is no tension. Sometimes it is very easy to live within both claims. Many of you are aware that I have at time studied and travelled in areas around the world that have opened my eyes and have made me more grateful for the fact that by accident of birth I was born in the United States. As one who spent a little time in the old Soviet Union, I am thankful for the privilege to vote, and have never once missed going to the polls. As a Presbyterian pastor I am grateful for my forebears, who led in the fight for freedom during the Revolutionary War, to the extent that in England the revolution was called "The Presbyterian Rebellion." As one who has been to Central America any number of times and talked with pastors who were victims of torture simply for preaching the Gospel, I am grateful for the freedom of the pulpit, which this grand church has always honored and which our nation has cherished. Many times, there is no tension in my attempt to live responsibly between the claims of citizenship and the claims of faithfulness.

But there are other times when I struggle with that tension. And this is one of those times. Our nation is on the verge of war. If the reports that I read are true, and if there is no unforeseen miracle breaking through, then it is my guess that within two weeks we will be in Iraq. There will be a new moon and thus safer to invade in the dark of night. It will be early enough to finish by the heat of summer. And the appropriate forces will be gathered on the border.

I have to admit it is a frightening time, more so than any other time in my life with the possible exception of the Cuban missile crisis in 1962 when the danger of nuclear weapons was 90 miles from our

135

shores. And as I have talked with many of you with a wide variety of perspectives, as I have read voraciously all that I could and talked with others around the nation, I have sensed that fear from others. I have found that there are a great number of people like me who have concerns about Saddam Hussein and his abuse of human rights, his production of chemical and biological weapons; we want to support the president because we have had enough divisiveness in our country through the years and there are so many other domestic issues that need our care, and yet there is an certain uneasiness…and fear… about the direction in which we are heading.

The faith community has been largely silent and that might be out of fear as well. Early on it was made clear from the President on down that those who questioned these policies were actually being disloyal…unpatriotic. And so I have been relatively silent. I have been silent because of my own uncertainty; I do not have the answers. And I have been silent because I have been afraid. I have grown to love you too much. I don't want to do anything that would get in the way of those relationships or hamper the growth and the excitement of a vibrant church.

You see, my friends, I don't have the courage of a T. K. Young who could, at great cost, stand in this pulpit and call for northern and southern Presbyterians to end the Civil War. I don't have the courage of a Paul Tudor Jones who could, at great cost, stand right here and declare "This is God's church…for all God's children." I certainly don't have the courage of a Dr. John Johnson, who walked the walk with the sanitation workers in 1968 seeking justice for those who wore signs saying "I am a man." I marvel at their courage and their leadership.

But in sorting out all these fears I realized that my greatest fear was that of not being true to what I believe is the meaning in our lives and central to our calling. It is the fear of standing for nothing important when there are alternatives to war. It is the fear of disloyalty to the promise of God, to the vision of a more graceful and compassionate life.

And so I come to you today not with the force of a "Thus saith the Lord," but rather with a "Come, let us reason together as troubled, struggling people of faith striving to do what is right and just." And as we struggle let us make sure that the first casualty of patriotism not be dissent, debate, and discussion. And though we might be of different minds on this matter, let us make sure that we are of one heart. Let us not challenge the patriotism of those who disagree with our current course, just as we not challenge the faith of those who favor military intervention. For if there is one thing we all have in common, it is that we share neither the mind nor the will of God, but the church must be the place where we use all of our resources to try to discern that mind and that will.

This process of discernment begins with the Bible, but not by simply taking a few verses here and a few verses there and making doctrines out of them. The Bible has been used to justify crusades and holy wars, based largely on the Old Testament, and it has been used to advocate pacifism, based largely on the teachings of Jesus. Rather, we take a look at the larger themes, and there can be little doubt that one of the predominate themes is God's will for shalom, peace, wholeness, health, visions of God's peaceable kingdom. Many of those visions are quite familiar to us: the lion laying down with the lamb; soldiers beating swords into plowshares, angelic chorus singing at Christmas "Peace on earth and good will to all; visions of a new heaven and a new earth where there will be no more pain.

The question confronts us, though: Do these visions of peace speak only of that day which is to come—or does it refer to reality now?

137

Were the prophets foolhardy idealists, impractical and other worldly? Or is it possible that they are the true realists? Do we trust the prophets' vision, or is that just so much utopian double talk with nothing to do with the hard realities of the way the world is?

Well, I don't know how you come down on that one. I confess to some ambivalence myself. But the first task of the Church is never to act, but to listen, to listen as faithfully and as obediently as one can to hear what the Word of the Lord is saying to the people of God.

Well, the word of the Lord given to us this day comes from Isaiah. It is written at one of the most critical moments in Israel's history. In 587 BC the armies of Babylon finally got tired of Israel being a thorn in their side and swooped down destroying the whole nation and sending Jerusalem up in smoke. Israel lost her Temple, her city, her nation, her land, her beloved land. It was not only a crisis of great political and cultural proportions, but it was especially a crisis of faith. They had been assured that they were the chosen people of God. God had been faithful from the time God promised that through Abraham all the families of the world would be blessed. And they had been blessed with divinely ordained kings in David and Solomon. God was on their side.

But now, with Jerusalem still smoldering from the fires of Babylon God had seemingly gone up in smoke with the Cedars of Lebanon that had been used to build the temple. And Israel just ends up as just another gimme in the win column of Babylon's schedule.

Isaiah does a strange thing. After recounting God's faithfulness to the people and saying as good as that story of the Exodus is, forget about it, because when it comes to the new thing that I (God) am doing, that old story won't mean a thing. "Do not remember the

138

former things nor consider the things of old. I am about to do a new thing."

Think of all God had done—making a way, a path in the mighty waters, causing the sea to close on the Egyptian pursuers. Yet God can do more. The important thing is to put your faith, your energy, and your will into the new thing that God is doing.

There is a challenge here for the people of faith, far removed from just putting our faith in a dreamy, apocalyptic vision for the end of time. This challenge is as earthy as water in the wilderness. The people must be open to the possibility of change and receptive to the opportunity to begin anew. They must not succumb to lethargy, or pride or cynicism, the old ways of doing things. Rather, they must stand straight, with their senses keen to perceive the advent of the god who comes to deliver slaves, to heal the sick, and to restore to wholeness that which is broken.

To claim that vision is to lean towards that vision, to work for that vision, is to put our hearts and minds and imaginations toward that vision; to will that vision. And if we end up invading Iraq, it will be because our imaginations have failed us.

We keep on hanging onto the old ways of doing things and not being open to the new things that God may be doing. We keep on debating ad nauseum the just war theory, and preachers and politicians will line up on either side, some arguing convincingly that this war is just. It meets all those criteria as it certainly did in World War II. Others arguing convincingly that there is no way that a pre-emptive war is just, and remind us that both sides in the Civil War claimed to be fighting for "just" causes, both invoking God's will. We dare not forget the belt buckles of German soldiers: Gott mitt uns. God is with us. Just wars are in the eyes of the beholders.

139

There is another problem with the just war theory. Augustine developed this doctrine over 1500 years ago when soldiers would meet on the battlefield. Those killed were, for the most part, soldiers. The theory was designed to limit the casualties to those fighting, sparing the lives of the innocent. For the next 1500 years that was more or less possible.

But we live in a new day. We had boasted that casualties in the first Persian Gulf war were limited, yet those were U.S. casualties. It has been only recently that the truth has come out. Over 35,000 civilians were killed during Desert Storm, and according to a UNICEF study, anywhere from 300,000 to 2 million children have died as a result of our bombing water supply and sewage treatment plants in Iraq after the Gulf War ended. According to the war plan called "Operation Shock and Awe" described in Newsweek, "in the first 48 hours of the attack the United States armed forces are expected to rain some 3,000 precision guided bombs and missiles" on Iraq. We can debate the intricacies of the Just War until we are blue in the face, but the problem is that a just war is no longer just a war.

In Isaiah God indeed does call us to remember, but not be trapped in those memories. Certainly there are lessons of history, but the lessons of history are also in the eyes of the beholder. We have heard the name Neville Chamberlain invoked, the passive naive trusting Prime Minister of England who signed a non-aggression pact with Hitler. Thus Great Britain was weak, unprepared. We make peace by preparing for war, we have been told ever since. But Neville Chamberlain was not the cause of World War II. The cause of World War II was World War I. Hitler's obsession was to avenge the humiliation of German people, caused both by the war and the inability of the world community to establish a just peace through the Treaty of Versailles.

Another lesson from that time concerned the churches. Christians could see no tension between the call to responsible citizenship and the call to faithful obedience to God. With but a few dissenters German Christians talked a great deal of "moral clarity": Listen to these words written in 1932:

"We want a living People's Church which is the expression of all the religious powers of our nation... We know something of the Christian duty and love toward the helpless, but we demand also the protection of the nation from the incapable and inferior... We want an Evangelical Church which roots in the national character."[1]

And thus the church became the religious arm of Hitler's regime. Moral clarity can so easily lead to moral arrogance, thus relegating the church to moral silence.

So what are we to do? Let Saddam have his way? One of the problems historically with the so-called peace movement is that we have not taken evil seriously. Reinhold Neibuhr reminded us of that a half a century ago. "The proper attitude toward evil is anger," he wrote. But we must avoid what Niebuhr saw as angers two temptations: hatred and vengeance and allow love, justice and integrity to shape our response to evil.

And our best hope for that response is the United Nations. Yes, I know its flaws and deficiencies well. But the veterans of World War II like Presidents Eisenhower and Kennedy who knew all too well the tragedy of war, opened their imaginations to a new order that used the United Nations effectively and for the most part, contained the Soviet Union, controlled the arms race and preserved the peace.

---

[1] From Shirley Guthrie, *Christian Doctrine: Revised Edition*, (Louisville, Kentucky, Westminster/John Knox Press, 1994) p. 21.

I think of the United Nations like Winston Churchill spoke of democracy: "Democracy is a poor form of government," he would say, "but there has been nothing invented that is better." The United Nations is what we have. And it could be so much stronger if we would pay the $1.2 billion in back dues we owe. That seems like a lot of money, but is miniscule compared to the $200 billion it has been estimated that a war, not to mention the aftermath, would cost.

When Robert Oppenheimer and his team first exploded the atom bomb that they had been working years on, he said "Everything has changed, except our way of thinking."

It is time for a new way of thinking. A way that affirms a strong patriotism, not short, frenzied outbursts of emotion, but the tranquil and steady dedication of a lifetime. But also a way that affirms that patriotism is not enough. A way that calls for us to be where God is. And what we know from the gospel is that God is on the cross, in the midst of the suffering of God's people. Wherever there is pain and death, God is there. Wherever there are lives being lost at the hands of ruthless tyrants, there stands the cross. Wherever evil rules the human heart and leads it to respond to evil with evil, there the Spirit of God weeps.

We are not without hope. For it was Abraham Lincoln, who in the midst of looking for a new way of thinking, told his fellow citizens: "The dogmas of the quiet past are inadequate to the stormy present. The occasion is piled high with difficulty and we must rise with the occasion. As our case is new, so we must think anew, and act anew. We must disenthrall ourselves, and then we shall save our country."

"Behold, I am about to do a new thing," says God.

Peace: A Mystery or Something Obvious?

July 7, 2013

(Preached in a Summer Sermon Series on Biblical and Theological Themes in Children's Books)

Luke 10:1-11

After this the Lord appointed seventy others and sent them on ahead of him in pairs to every town and place where he himself intended to go. 2He said to them, "The harvest is plentiful, but the laborers are few; therefore ask the Lord of the harvest to send out laborers into his harvest. 3Go on your way. See, I am sending you out like lambs into the midst of wolves. 4Carry no purse, no bag, no sandals; and greet no one on the road. 5Whatever house you enter, first say, 'Peace to this house!' 6And if anyone is there who shares in peace, your peace will rest on that person; but if not, it will return to you. 7Remain in the same house, eating and drinking whatever they provide, for the laborer deserves to be paid. Do not move about from house to house. 8Whenever you enter a town and its people welcome you, eat what is set before you; 9cure the sick who are there, and say to them, 'The kingdom of God has come near to you.' 10But whenever you enter a town and they do not welcome you, go out into its streets and say, 11 'Even the dust of your town that clings to our feet, we wipe off in protest against you. Yet know this: the kingdom of God has come near.'

Prayer of Illumination: O God, in Jesus Christ you sent the Prince of Peace, which we celebrate in the midst of a cold December. On this warm July Sunday, open our hearts, our ears, and my mouth, that we might be startled to discover anew what it means to follow him. Amen.

143

RECENTLY, DAVID BROOKS, A COLUMNIST FROM the New York Times, wrote a piece describing how the folks at Google released a database of 5.2 million books published between 1500 and 2008. You simply type a search word into the database and find out how frequently different words were used at different epochs. It doesn't tell you how the words were used; it just tells you how frequently they were used.

There were some studies Brooks highlighted that had been done about word usage over the past half century, which he, and I, found to be discomforting. One study found that between 1960 and 2008, individualistic words and phrases increasingly overshadowed communal words and phrases.

That is to say, over those 48 years, words and phrases like "personalized," "self," "unique," "I can do it myself," and "I come first" were used more frequently. Communal words and phrases like "community," "share," "united," "band together," and "common good" receded.

There was a second part of that study that had to do with moral terms. Words like "decency," "virtue," and "conscience," have been used less and less over the past half century. Words like "honesty," "patience," and "compassion" likewise fell dramatically in their use. Usage of gratitude words like "thankfulness" and "appreciation" dropped by 48%. Use of compassion words like "kindness" and "helpfulness" dropped by 56%.

These studies highlight the growing sense of individualism in our country (What's in it for me?"), the increasing distrust of the other (those that aren't like me), fostering a growing frag-mentation, polarization, and alienation from each other; That in turn can very easily lead to a demonization of the other, ("You're not just wrong, you're evil!") and we know what that leads to.

On this Fourth of July week-end, I remain in awe of the thread of continuity in our national identity—institutions, ideas, and attitude that remains unbroken. Above all, we are still, at root, a nation that believes in democracy, even if we don't always act on that belief. That's a remark-able thing when you consider how much our country has changed in the past 237 years.

But still, those language trends are troubling this birthday weekend... So the question I have is "Can we change that? Can an entire society learn to think differently about our interrelated-ness? About the common good? That we are all in this thing called "life" together? Can we embrace a more global patriotism, a love for all the nations of the world, their children, the lilies of their fields, the birds of their air, the fish of their seas, no less than our love for our nation, our children, our lilies of the field, birds of the air, our fish of the sea?" I think we can, but nothing short of a whole different way of thinking—different language, different purpose, and different goals—will save us. And here's the good news:

Jesus believes it can be done. Jesus has prepared us for that, and has given us marching orders. It was a harsh world that Jesus and his followers lived in. Oh, we've heard a lot about the Pax Romana, the Peace of Rome, but there was no peace. When a city rebelled, like Carthage, the empire burned it and plowed it under, and they called it peace. They built highways and aqua-ducts and fostered trade and spread commerce, and they called it peace.

But the heavy boot of Rome was on the necks of the peasants in Palestine...Galileans, Judeans, Samaritans, and Rome's military presence made it stay that way. They would line the highways with bodies up on crosses to serve as reminders to those who disobeyed. Can you imagine what it must have been like to have been a young woman, walking to the market, past the sneering Roman soldiers, knowing what they did to women and girls? And some of the Jews were ready to revolt. They were called the Zealots, and at least one of Jesus' disciples, Simon, was one of these rebels, ready for an armed insurrection, to meet force with force, violence with more violence.

So as Jesus went about the countryside, preaching good news to the poor, proclaiming release to the captives, restoring sight to the blind, and reminding people that the Kingdom of God has come near, it all sounded so harmless, but it was threatening. He had noticed that the more he healed, the more he preached the gospel of peace, and the more opposition arose. And so, in this poignant scene today, he realizes that he can't do it alone, and he prepares not the 12 as he had done before, but 70 followers to go out into the world. 70. Hmm. 70. Might that refer to the table of nations in Genesis 10, which stands for all of humanity, and not just Israel? He didn't send them with travel guides and Conde Nast magazines, places to eat. They were not going as conquering consumers, or confident crusaders, but as lambs in the midst of wolves.

He gave them no practical advice about how to order a meal or find a room. Travel light, he said. No purse. No bag. No sandals. And he gave them a word. When they entered a household, say "Peace. "Peace be to this house." Sounds harmless enough. Who can be against peace? We say it easily when we greet one another at the passing of the peace (or at least most of us do!)

But this passage makes clear that in our world then and now, peace is shunned, feared, and rejected—not just peace as the absence of war, but that peace which is wholeness and blessing. To live in peace is to live in right relationship with God and then, inevitably, with our sisters and brothers as well, and indeed, with all of creation. To live at peace is to let go of our unloveliness and our unlovingness, to put self and individualism aside and to enter into wholeness.

And Jesus knew that when we said "peace," when we made peace our priority, we would experience woundedness and rejection. Some of the most vehement responses to sermons I have had through the years have not been over issues of sexuality or poverty or racism or any other "hot" topics, but when I have tried to proclaim a gospel of peace in the midst of war or preparation for war. So Jesus gives us further instructions, when one is rejected, when the gospel of peace does stir up fear and hostility, don't pull out the dagger. Do not respond in kind. Let your manner be peaceful. Dust off your feet, he says, move on, and remember, the Kingdom of God has come near.

The world, of course, didn't get it. Jesus is only recorded twice in scripture as weeping. One time was when his friend Lazarus died. The other time was that poignant scene in the final week of his life. As he prepared to ride the donkey into Jerusalem, as the crowds were waiting for him to make the move, to claim his inheritance as King, he stopped, and looked over the city and wept. Why? Because, Luke tells us, they did not know the things that made for peace. He didn't say what made for peace. He chose to make it a mystery; or was it so obvious?

One of my favorite stories as a child was the story of Ferdinand the Bull. I didn't know until later when that was written: in Spain, in 1936, in the midst of a violent Civil War, which makes this story all the more remarkable.

Do you remember Ferdinand? He was no ordinary bull. He saw things differently. Unlike all the other bulls in history and tradition, the great symbol of strength, aggression, violence, and warfare, Ferdinand preferred the peaceful life of harmony and tranquility where he could enjoy the trees and the flowers. As the years went by, Ferdinand grew into a very large and ferocious looking bull.

One day, when the men came from Madrid, scouting for the most spirited beasts they could find in order to take them back for the famous bullfights, they found Ferdinand in the field with all the other young bulls. While the others, eager to be chosen, put on the most ferocious display, Ferdinand was content to sit in the corner of the field smelling the flowers and watching the show.

Only, as Ferdinand sat down, he had the misfortune to sit on a bumble bee which stung him mercilessly, where upon Ferdinand rose with great roar and began charging about, snorting and bellowing, butting the air and pawing the ground in a way that impressed the scouts tremendously. So impressed, they took Ferdinand to Madrid for the great bullfight. On the day of the contest, a great crowd assembled, for it was said that Ferdinand was the fiercest bull in all Spain.

Only, when the gate was opened and Ferdinand strolled into the center of the ring, amid the wild cheers of the crowd, he smelled the lovely flowers in the hair of all the ladies. And Ferdinand calmly sat down to enjoy it all. Nothing the matadors could do would make Ferdinand fight. They hit him, screamed at him, waved their red flags, poked him, but Ferdinand refused to fight, preferring the peacefulness of the spring day and the beautiful flowers. And so finally they took him back to the pasture, where, the author wrote, "he sits to this day under his favorite cork tree, smelling the flowers. He is very happy."

In the wisdom of a child's story we get a clue about the ultimate question of peace and salvation, for it raises the question: Where is true life to be found? For the other bulls, life was to be found in Madrid, in the bull fight. Only Ferdinand saw things differently. Ferdinand noticed things the others did not notice, the simple pleasures of the pasture, the humble beauty of the flowers, the trees, the butterflies. In a world influenced by things that do not make for peace, the story offers alternative norms: stillness, harmony, creation, and peace.

And the remarkable thing about Ferdinand is that although he is no hero, he is a very remarkable bull. Oh, he performs none of those marvelous feats that might give him a name and turn him into a stirring legend. He climbs no mountains, slays no dragons, rescues no maidens, makes no riches, and leads no mighty army. Yet in something that is so obvious, he is already where the hero is trying to valiantly to get.

"Peace be to this house." Jesus did not spell out the things that made for peace as he looked out over the city and wept on his parade. Was it because it was such a deep mystery; or is it so obvious?

The docile, peaceful Ferdinand already possessed what the other warring bulls were fighting for. The only difference between that lovely story and the Gospel is that children hear that story and laugh. We read the gospel and the newspaper and we weep because we do not know the things that make for peace.

So can we change? Can we change how we think about peace? Can we glorify peace as much as we do war? We have changed how we think about child labor, about slavery. We have changed how as a society we think about segregation. But let us not delude ourselves into thinking racism has been abolished. We have changed how we think about the role of women, although I warn you, there is a backlash developing. We are changing how we think about full equality for gays and lesbians. We have more work to do on those.

But Jesus believed we CAN change. We can be more compassionate and kinder. We can as a church promote the "common good," and ask for God's blessing upon all the nations of the world. We can be thankful. For Jesus not only gave us the right words to use "Peace be to this house." But after entering the city, one night he gave us more. This is my body. This is my blood. This is where peace can begin. But the Gospel demands that we not let it end here.

Amen.

Stephen
May 22, 2011

Acts 7:55-8:3

55 But filled with the Holy Spirit, he gazed into heaven and saw the glory of God and Jesus standing at the right hand of God. 56 "Look," he said, "I see the heavens opened and the Son of Man standing at the right hand of God!" 57 But they covered their ears, and with a loud shout all rushed together against him. 58 Then they dragged him out of the city and began to stone him; and the witnesses laid their coats at the feet of a young man named Saul. 59 While they were stoning Stephen, he prayed, "Lord Jesus, receive my spirit." 60 Then he knelt down and cried out in a loud voice, "Lord, do not hold this sin against them." When he had said this, he died.

1 And Saul approved of their killing him. That day a severe persecution began against the church in Jerusalem, and all except the apostles were scattered throughout the countryside of Judea and Samaria. 2 Devout men buried Stephen and made loud lamentation over him. 3 But Saul was ravaging the church by entering house after house; dragging off both men and women, he committed them to prison.

Prayer: We thank you for this bright and beautiful day; for the time to be together; for friends with whom to worship; for a church to nurture our faith and call for our commitment; and for a sense of your lively presence. Now startle us with your truth and your word, in Jesus Christ our Lord. Amen.

DESPITE THE TITLE OF THE SERMON, it's not all about me! However, in rereading this story of Stephen and what his obedience to Jesus Christ cost him, I was reminded of a poem that was written by one of my parishioners, June Shore, when I was first ordained over 30 years ago in Buckhorn, Kentucky:

> You must involve the wary teens—their needs must be attended,
>
> But not to such a great extent that the old guard be offended.
>
> Take care in quoting from the Greek, lest you be thought "uptown,"
>
> Yet should you wax too folksy, you'll offend by "talking down."
>
> With sermons swift and to the point, you short-change your little flock;
>
> Yet discuss a theme quite fully, and you're competing with the clock.
>
> And if you preach salvation, you'll be slighting social action;
>
> But if you march for peace and love, you'll offend the Jesus faction.
>
> The budget must be balanced, though the dollar takes a drubbing;

Yet some think the tithing texts are just too "money grubbing."

Your dress should reflect at all times the dignity of your calling,

But wear the congregational Christmas ties, no matter how appalling!

Be a sport (but not a clown) to appease the community sector,

And wherever you go, don't tread on the toe of the venerable choir director!

In view of such behavior from the ecclesiastical mob,

And in terms of pay and work load, can't you find a better job?

Let it be said that not only has this ecclesiastical mob never threatened to stone this Stephen, one could not be more blessed to be the pastor of such a faithful and supportive group of followers of Jesus Christ. You continue to inspire and amaze me.

Today's story is of the stoning of Stephen, something I've never preached on before, partly because I didn't know what to say that would do it justice. But as I shared with you recently, I have been spending a lot of time with the early church in scriptures over the past few weeks, and I began to read this passage with new eyes. Because this is not only about what happens to Stephen, the very first Christian martyr, but also about what happens to a young man who is watching and approving and keeping an eye on the coats of those who are stoning him. And it is indeed a reminder that vocations—all vocations—can be costly as well as blessed; that there are no guarantees that good work will be rewarded appropriately every time.

Let me set the stage: Earlier in Acts, Peter stands before a crowd in Jerusalem on Solomon's Portico, and preaches a sermon. Just like that 3,000 are converted! And the Luke, who wrote Acts, tells us how that early Christian community "spent much time together in the temple, they broke bread at home … praising God and having the goodwill of all the people. And day by day, the Lord added to their number those who were being saved." That's a pretty good start for a group that only months before had been a tiny, frightened group of disciples hiding behind closed doors.

But there were growing pains, as there always are. It's one thing to be a loose-knit band of disciples walking from synagogue to synagogue in Galilee. It's another thing to be over 3,000 strong, cramming Jerusalem streets with no building, no organization, no staff, no computers, and no stewardship campaign. Nothing, really, except a newly born passionate faith.

One of the first things they did was to get organized, not to have a revival or start a television ministry, but to make sure that everyone had enough to eat. That's admirable, but a formidable task, because in their lack of organization, some weren't getting fed, especially the Greek speaking converts, and they complain that the new church has to do something: get organized, form some committees, find some new leaders, and put them to work.

That's where Stephen enters the story. He is not, like Peter, one of the original 12 apostles. Luke simply says that he is a man full of faith and the Holy Spirit, and he is selected as a deacon ordained to the work of waiting tables, taking care of the widow, and the daily distribution of the bread.

It wasn't long, however, before everything they did became a hotbed of controversy (as things in Jerusalem, it seems have always been, even today!) Some Jewish leaders got into an argument with Stephen and they threw the book at him: blasphemy, sedition, and all the old charges that people bring up when they feel threatened and afraid. They charged that he had slandered Moses and "the law" and God and the temple; and that this Jesus he followed would change the customs instituted by Moses too radically; so he was dragged before the high priest and the council. He didn't have adequate legal advice like he would today; for if he had, his lawyers would have told him to keep his mouth shut.

He didn't. Stephen began to preach an ill-advised sermon before the judges. It was a bible lesson going all the way back to Abraham. "You have your nerve to charge that I have violated Moses and his law— Get a mirror: look at you!" He works his way through the holy history of God's saving activity. Even as far back as Joseph there was conflict already within the family of Abraham. He recounts the story of Moses in loving detail and awe. He was demonstrating anything but blasphemy, but he reminds them that even Moses in his day got little affection, for even his own people refused to obey him.

Then he explains how Jesus was put to death by the very people who were sitting in front of him, that they bore the stain of Jesus' blood. And then he ended by saying something that any preaching professor would warn him against saying: "You're a bunch of stiff-necked people, forever opposing the Holy Spirit, persecuting the prophets."

Needless to say, Stephen's sermon (the longest in Acts) had a different result than Peter's sermon (which produced 3,000 converts). There were no converts this day, no community that arose to live in harmony, no goodwill that resulted in mission. Instead, the council rushed on Stephen, dragging him from the temple and taking him outside the city's wall where they stoned him to death.

In these two contrasting stories, we get a picture of how the early church developed, inspired by the Holy Spirit, and manifested in the witnesses of both of these early disciples, the one through successful efforts leading to a new church development, the other to martyrdom in the manner of Jesus himself.

The church didn't sustain those early joyful days very long. As a matter of fact, remember the economic plan to sell goods and feed people? It turns out that Ananias and his wife Sapphira embezzled some of the funds and then lied to the apostles about the money. And Luke reports that Ananias, and then a bit later Sapphira suffered cardiac arrest—Luke contends that the stealing and lying, and the subsequent deaths were not coincidental. I remember seeing a church that advertised itself on a billboard as a "New Testament church." I wonder if they mean dishonesty, scandal, or martyrdom.

Now here's what I really wonder: why did Luke put all these awkward stories in there? They're embarrassing. Church leaders stealing? Leaders of the church being thrown in jail? Could you see the annual report? "We're very proud of our leaders this year who were arrested in early January and were flogged just prior to their release." And Stephen? Though I like the name, he was intemperate, uncompromising, and used poor judgment about when and how to share his personal witness to Jesus Christ. He was ordained simply to feed poor people and wait on tables!

And yet they are in the Bible, preserved as the work of the Holy Spirit. Luke, I think, wants to show that the Spirit was guiding the church through it all, and is guiding it still.

But there is a footnote here, perhaps another reason that Luke felt called to write this down. When Stephen was martyred, there was a man there by the name of Saul who looked on with glee and held the coats of those who were stoning Stephen. Saul was filled with hatred for the Christians. This is the same Saul who later became Paul, converted on the Damascus road, the first and indisputably the greatest Christian theologian of them all. Saul would never forget what he heard that day, a young, faithful man dying for his convictions, praying with his last breath a paraphrase of an old Jewish evening prayer: "Lord, receive my spirit." Only Stephen prayed "Lord Jesus, receive my spirit," as he died. Stephen forgave his executioners and Saul never forgot that. Augustine suggested that "If Stephen had not prayed, the Church would not have had Paul." Who of us is ever aware of what the Holy Spirit is doing in the church?

So why did Luke include this story of the first martyr? Some think he included it to show how Stephen was a model Christian. I'm sure that was compelling for the early Christians, just as compelling as Archbishop Oscar Romero and nuns and priests who gave their lives for the faith in El Salvador. But I think there was another reason. I think Luke wanted to identify the thread of the presence of God's Spirit that runs through the story of the church in good times and bad, when the church grows by leaps and bounds, with great preaching and 3,000 converts, breaking bread in the homes, praying in the temple. But also in those times when those who are full of faith and filled with the Holy Spirit fall into the hands of deceitful people, dishonest people, taken outside the city and stoned, cloaks thrown at the feet of a hater of the church who will become one of its greatest leaders.

God has a way of working through it all, don't you see? Of turning it all around, of taking great tragedy and somehow fashioning newness and hope. God's Spirit is with us in everything the church has been and will be; in the great shining moments of harmony and growth and peace, (like last week with 10 new members and a baptism and a party on the playground) and in the wrenching sadness that brings sorrow upon the church. And yes, it's important for every one of us to realize that the church is an imperfect vessel, at times gossipy, petty, falling apart, torn by controversy and doctrinal dispute, subject to error at times when it strays from the Spirit of God. And yet always, always called back to witness to and exemplify the resurrection life of Jesus Christ of which on earth it is his body.

Look at it this way: All God has to work with are the likes of you and me, the Stephens and Stephanies, the Pauls and the Paulines of today. And there will be times we will blow it, maybe say the wrong things at the wrong times to the wrong people, to get ourselves into jams we can't seem to get out of, to take our assigned tasks and not do it as well as some others might.

But that is no reason not to try, not to do our best to be the church God has called us to be, imperfect as we are. For the Spirit is at work within us in ways perceptible and imperceptible and who knows save God alone what the end of these things will be? And if we look carefully, very carefully, even in these uncertain times, we will see the unmistakable movement of the Holy Spirit.

No, this story of Stephen is not about me. It is about all of us who are called to be disciples of Jesus Christ, and I, for one, wouldn't trade that calling for anything in the world. Amen.

The Bible: Literally or Seriously?

October 20, 2013

2 Timothy 3:14-4:5

14But as for you, continue in what you have learned and firmly believed, knowing from whom you learned it, 15and how from childhood you have known the sacred writings that are able to instruct you for salvation through faith in Christ Jesus. 16All scripture is inspired by God and is useful for teaching, for reproof, for correction, and for training in righteousness, 17so that everyone who belongs to God may be proficient, equipped for every good work.

4In the presence of God and of Christ Jesus, who is to judge the living and the dead, and in view of his appearing and his kingdom, I solemnly urge you: 2proclaim the message; be persistent whether the time is favorable or unfavorable; convince, rebuke, and encourage, with the utmost patience in teaching. 3For the time is coming when people will not put up with sound doctrine, but having itching ears, they will accumulate for themselves teachers to suit their own desires, 4and will turn away from listening to the truth and wander away to myths. 5As for you, always be sober, endure suffering, do the work of an evangelist, carry out your ministry fully.

Prayer: Startle us, O God, with your truth, and open our minds and hearts to your word, that hearing we may believe, and believing, we might trust you with our lives. Through Jesus Christ our Lord. Amen.

OVER THE PAST FEW YEARS, THERE HAVE been two books that have been written by authors who have attempted to take the Bible literally. Both have become best sellers. The first one was written by A.J. Jacobs, who describes himself as a secular Jew. The title was *A Year of Living Biblically*.

For one year, he lived by the rules and regulations and teachings of the Bible. For example, in accordance with Deuteronomy 22, he engaged the services of a New York shatnez tester to ensure that his clothes did not mix wool and linen in them. In accordance with Exodus 23, he removed the names of false gods from his vocabulary, which meant that he could not even use the words "Wednesday" and "Thursday" because they honor the false gods Woden and Thor. He allowed the side of his hair to grow uncut in accordance with Leviticus 19 and wore all white garments (Ecclesiastes 9:8). Fortunately, he did not have a son. I wonder what he would have done with this, from Deuteronomy: "If anyone has a stubborn and rebellious son, who will not obey the voice of the father or mother… then they shall take him out to the elders… at the gate of the place where he lives… Then all the men of the city shall stone him to death."

A.J. Jacobs' point, however, seemed clear: The Bible is an outdated, irrelevant dinosaur of antiquity, not to be taken seriously, but rather humorously, especially if there were royalties involved.

There was another book that just came out last year, this time written by someone within the faith. And not just the faith, but the evangelical Christian faith that nurtured her as a child.

Rachel Held Evans' book title said it all: *A Year of Biblical Womanhood: How a Liberated Woman Found Herself Sitting on her roof, Covering Her Head, and Calling her Husband 'Master.'*

She had been taught to take the Bible seriously, and even literally on some points, but when she got to college, a "Christian" college, she began to realize how selective Christians are when we try to live "biblically." It started in dormitory late night sessions over whether God wanted young ladies at a Christian college to run for student body president. Some said that Paul, in writing to Timothy, authored rules about biblical women stepping aside to allow godly men to take the lead.

She said that some argued that those instructions only applied within the church, not the college. Others said that there weren't a whole lot of godly men beating down the doors to plan banquets and pep rallies that year.

So the concept of "biblical womanhood" intrigued her. Because she still held the Bible to be authoritative, the very word of God. And yet, technically speaking, it was biblical for a woman to be sold by her father (Exodus 21:7); biblical for her to be forced to marry her rapist (Dt. 22:28-29); biblical for her to remain silent in church (I Cor. 14:34-35), biblical for her to cover her head (I Cor. 11:6), and biblical for her to be one of multiple wives. Was there one biblical formula for how to be a woman... and a Christian? Unlike Jacobs, she asked this question as an insider.

So Rachel lived for a year, along with her husband Dan, who emerged as a real saint, in pursuit of true biblical womanhood. Each month she took a different directive from scripture and tried to be true to them by attaching goals to each. One month she focused on domesticity..."She watched over the affairs of her household...," Proverbs describes the "ideal" woman, and so Rachel cooked through Martha Stewart's Cooking School, as well as performing other domestic chores. The next month she was obedient... even called her husband "master" throughout December.

161

(Incidentally, this book has actually spawned a church school class of women, some of whom have been baptized in this church and others who grew up in churches in which women were not allowed to teach, or preach, or serve as officers.)

Though both of these books are somewhat light-hearted, they raise a basic question about the Bible: How are we to read it? What are we to make of those difficult passages that were written anywhere from -2,000 to 3,000 years ago. I don't think we at Idlewild are content with the bumper sticker "The Bible says it; I believe it. That settles it."

And the Bible itself gives very little insight as to how to read the Bible. The Psalms talk about the importance of the law, "How I love thy law O Lord." But the closest thing we have to instructions are found in a tender letter written by Paul to his beloved friend, Timothy, in what is considered the last of Paul's letters written from a prison cell in Rome on the eve of his death.

Timothy had been raised in the faith by his mother Eunice and his grandmother Lois in Lystra.

(That alone is often forgotten by many pastors.) Taught by Paul, nurtured by the elders and teachers of the community, theirs was a close relationship, and Paul felt a strong connection to Timothy. You hear it in the warm and personal greetings Paul writes, "Timothy, my dearly beloved son, I long to see you day and night, that I may be filled with joy."

It is a letter written with much pathos, a touching exchange between dear friends. And it is no less touching that Paul ends the letter by saying to Timothy, "I am already on the point of being sacrificed, the time of my departure has come. I have fought the good fight, I have finished the race, and I have kept the faith."

Paul wants, in his final days, to give some words of encouragement to Timothy, whom he knew would suffer as well because of his devotion to Christ. And what does Paul say?"

Continue in what you have learned… knowing from whom you learned it, and how from childhood you have known the sacred writings, that are able to instruct you for salvation through Christ Jesus. All scripture is inspired by God and is useful for teaching, for reproof, for correction, and for training in righteousness.

Now, when Paul refers to scripture, we need to know that he is not referring to scripture as we know it…66 books bound up into one volume. The canon as we know it was to come hundreds of years later. He was talking about the Torah (the first five books of our Old Testament), the prophets, and the Psalms. Paul believed that these scriptures pointed the way to the one they knew in Jesus Christ as the fulfillment of their messianic.

My heart goes out to Paul as he offers what advice he gives to Timothy as his "last will and testament." But really, can we affirm with Paul that all scripture is useful for teaching… for training in righteousness?

Psalm 137? "Happy shall they be who take your little ones and dash them against the rock!"

The Holiness Code in Leviticus? I won't even go there.

What about the unquestioning assumption of slavery? The first letter of Peter advises, "Slaves, accept the authority of your masters with all deference, not only those who are kind and gentle but also those who are harsh." Is this the enduring Christian perspective on slavery?

Peter Gomes, who until his death a few years ago was the chaplain at Harvard, wrote in his book, *The Good Book*, about the African American theologian Howard Thurman, whose grandmother in her girlhood had been a slave. She had been taught to read and write, and she knew much of the Bible by heart. It was she who taught her grandson the scriptures.

When Thurman got to seminary and began to study the Bible on his own, he discovered that his grandmother had never said anything about St. Paul. He asked her why, and she replied that when the black slave preacher came he would preach about Moses and Jesus. But when the white preacher came once a month he always preached from Ephesians 6:5, where St. Paul says, "Slaves be obedient to those who are your earthly masters…' When she got to read the scriptures for herself, she took her scissors and cut out all of Pauls' writings from the New Testament on the grounds that they were inconsistent with what Jesus taught, and therefore had no place in the Bible. Now Gomes did not approve of this practice. He labeled it the excessive zeal of culturalism, which sustains and validates in the name of God the prejudices of a parochial community. But we can understand the temptation of Thurman's grandmother to excise from the Bible that what she knew from her own experience to be untrue.

As we receive the Bible's instruction, we have to acknowledge that this is a book some portions of which we can embrace as life sustaining and life giving, a guidebook to living a whole life.

While other portions of it will cause us to enter into an argument, a teaching that goes against the grain of all that we know to be right and true and even holy. Knowing which is which is the business of a lifelong enterprise of engagement, conversation, disagreement, study, and wonderment. That is the Presbyterian understanding of how we are meant to encounter the Bible.

There are some passages of scripture that are so horrible that they invite us to do nothing so much as move on, particularly some of the extremely violent scenes, which are especially hard to read given the sub-culture of war and violence today. Some parts of the Bible are troublesome and some parts are soaring in their beauty, inspiration, and power.

I want to make a case today for taking the Bible seriously, not literally, but for making the Bible your source book for a lifetime of spiritual growth and study. I have to admit that nothing has grated on me like the accusations of those who left our denomination because, in their words, "We did not take the Bible authoritatively." That was bearing false witness against me, and Idlewild, as well as the Presbyterian Church (USA).There have to be some guidelines, of course, and we Presbyterians have a few:

First, (and I am indebted to one of my teachers of Bible, Kendra Hotz, for this) pay attention to context, context, and context. What was going on surrounding this particular story or text?

What was the culture like? Then, what was going on when it was written, sometimes hundreds of years later? Why was it written included in scripture? And finally, our own context. What do we bring to bear to the readings? What experiences, what cultural prejudices do we have that shape our reading?

One of the sad ironies of the southern church, primarily Baptist but also Presbyterian, is that southern churches stressed knowing the

Bible. Christian Education was one of the two major priorities of the Southern Presbyterian Church… mission being the other. But it was these same churches that were not able to see how their own culture blinded them to the evils of slavery or segregation, so when they approached the Bible, they could cite chapter and verse, but missed the gospel.

Which is related to another guideline. When we read the Bible, all of our interpretations should be in accord with the "rule of love." What does this text mean in light of Jesus' two fold commandment to love God and to love neighbor? In short, this means that if someone interprets scripture in a way that is demeaning to God or hurtful to people, we need to question that interpretation. If our interpretation causes us to exclude or demean or demonize others, then there is probably something wrong about what we believe is right. We read the scriptures through the lens of the love of Christ.

Third, when we study scriptures, we do it with others, especially those who might be different from us, who might have different life experiences from us. I know that when I, as a white, privileged, North American male sits down with Pastor Dan from Ghana, or Pastor Alison from Cuba, or Pastors Gayle, Anne and Margaret, or anyone not in a position of power or authority, then my eyes are opened to a greater truth that I could ever have imagined by myself, or with other white privileged, male Presbyterian pastors. Some of you have heard me say that my greatest spiritual and intellectual growth has always come from people who are different from me, or disagree with me. That's why I love Idlewild so.

The final guideline, or gift, that we need to bring to the table when we study scripture is that of humility. Humility. I need to be open to the possibility that I might be wrong about my interpretation. I need to take seriously the objections of those who disagree with me. For

I do not have a corner on truth, Presbyterians do not have a corner on truth. Jesus promised his followers that the Holy Spirit would lead them into a deeper understanding of the truth. There is always more light to be shed upon our study. There is always something new. "I am about to do a new thing," God said in Isaiah. And it takes humility and an openness to the Holy Spirit to be a part of that newness.

At the end of his book A.J. Jacobs, definitely not a Presbyterian, learned that he could not interpret the Bible alone. So every day he met with others to discuss its meaning. It drew him into community and into a new way of thinking of others. For the first time he considered the possibility that there is One who created us, and soon he felt a connection to the whole human family. By the end, Jacobs went from being an atheistic, secular Jew, to a "reverent agnostic."

And as for Rachel Held Evans, her faith was strengthened. She still loves the church and is thankful for her evangelical nurturing, though she became more aware of its shortcomings. At the end she wrote 10 resolutions, and the last one surprised her. "Keep loving, studying, and struggling with the Bible—because no matter how hard I fight it, it will always call me back."

And so we baptized little Kate today. I hope that Casey and Ali are comforted with the realization that they will not be alone in raising her and nurturing her in the love of God. For you have made vows as well. The nurture begins, I suppose, with the poignant words from a man about to die, imparting to his beloved friend what was really important:

All scripture is inspired by God and is useful for teaching, for reproof, for correction, and for training in righteousness, so that

167

everyone who belongs to God may be proficient, equipped for every good work.

If we take our vows seriously, then Kate will learn the most important thing that she will ever know...

"Jesus loves me, this I know

For the Bible tells me so."

Thanks be to God.

[1] A.J. Jacobs, *The Year of Living Biblically* (New York: Simon and Schuster, 2007).

[2] Rachel Held Evans, *A Year of Biblical Womanhood: How a Liberated Woman Found Herself Sitting on her Roof, Covering her Head, and Calling Her Husband "Master."* (Nashville: Thomas Nelson, 2012.

[3] Peter Gomes, *The Good Book: Reading the Bible with Mind and Heart,* (New York: William Morrow and Co.,

The Dignity of Difference: Presbyterians and Jews

November 21, 2004

Deuteronomy 26:1-11; Ephesians 3:1-12

When you have come into the land that the Lord your God is giving you as an inheritance to possess, and you possess it, and settle in it, 2you shall take some of the first of all the fruit of the ground, which you harvest from the land that the Lord your God is giving you, and you shall put it in a basket and go to the place that the Lord your God will choose as a dwelling for his name. 3You shall go to the priest who is in office at that time, and say to him, "Today I declare to the Lord your God that I have come into the land that the Lord swore to our ancestors to give us." 4When the priest takes the basket from your hand and sets it down before the altar of the Lord your God, 5you shall make this response before the Lord your God: "A wandering Aramean was my ancestor; he went down into Egypt and lived there as an alien, few in number, and there he became a great nation, mighty and populous. 6When the Egyptians treated us harshly and afflicted us, by imposing hard labor on us, 7we cried to the Lord, the God of our ancestors; the Lord heard our voice and saw our affliction, our toil, and our oppression. 8The Lord brought us out of Egypt with a mighty hand and an outstretched arm, with a terrifying display of power, and with signs and wonders; 9and he brought us into this place and gave us this land, a land flowing with milk and honey. 10So now I bring the first of the fruit of the ground that you, O Lord, have given me." You shall set it down before the Lord your God and bow down before the Lord your God. 11Then you, together with the Levites and the aliens who reside among you, shall celebrate with all the bounty that the Lord your God has given to you and to your house.

This is the reason that I Paul am a prisoner for Christ Jesus for the sake of you Gentiles— 2for surely you have already heard of the commission of God's grace that was given me for you, 3and how the mystery was made known to me by revelation, as I wrote above in a few words, 4a reading of which will enable you to perceive my understanding of the mystery of Christ. 5In former generations this mystery was not made known to humankind, as it has now been revealed to his holy apostles and prophets by the Spirit: 6that is, the Gentiles have become fellow heirs, members of the same body, and sharers in the promise in Christ Jesus through the gospel. 7Of this gospel I have become a servant according to the gift of God's grace that was given me by the working of his power. 8Although I am the very least of all the saints, this grace was given to me to bring to the Gentiles the news of the boundless riches of Christ, 9and to make everyone see what is the plan of the mystery hidden for ages in God who created all things; 10so that through the church the wisdom of God in its rich variety might now be made known to the rulers and authorities in the heavenly places. 11This was in accordance with the eternal purpose that he has carried out in Christ Jesus our Lord, 12in whom we have access to God in boldness and confidence through faith in him.

Prayer: O God, as you have walked with us through the past, accompany us into the future, shaping our thoughts to appreciate truth, justice, purity, holiness, and the magnificent oneness of your whole creation. Amen.

WHEN I FIRST ARRIVED HERE IN AUGUST, 2000, about two days after we had set up our phone connection in our home, I received my first phone call. It was from someone named Micah Greenstein, who introduced himself as the rabbi at Temple Israel, and said we had some common friends and just wanted to welcome me to Memphis. It was the first contact I had had with any other clergy, so I jumped at the chance to have lunch with him over at Finos. "How will I know you?" he asked. "I'm the one who looks like a rabbi," I told him.

Over the past four years one of the most precious relationships I have had here in Memphis has been my relationship with Micah, and also with the wonderful folks at Temple Israel. I have often said that I shudder to think of what Memphis would be like without Idlewild's faithful witness through the years. But I can't even dare to imagine how much poorer spiritually we would be were it not for the faithful presence of Temple Israel through the years...150 of them! Many of you know of how Rabbi Wax pushed for justice and reconciliation between races and religions in the 1950's and 60's and 70's; but he did not start that tradition.

When Rabbi Max Samfield died in 1915, his heroism during the yellow fever epidemics, which inspired and gave hope to an entire city, led the Memphis Street Railway Company to cut off its power during the rabbi's funeral as a gesture of unprecedented respect, causing every streetcar in town to come to a halt for a full minute. This, incidentally was roughly at the same time of the lynching of Leo Frank, a young Jewish man in Georgia. Tensions were high, making this gesture all the more remarkable. Rabbi Samfield's successor, Rabbi William Fineshriber, became the first clergy person in the city to condemn the Ku Klux Klan as early as 1921, a very dangerous thing to do at that point, but he was the first.

How much poorer we would be spiritually were it not for our brothers and sisters at Temple Israel. Most recently, there has been a group of members from Idlewild and Temple Israel who have just completed an intensive study together entitled "Open Doors, Open Minds," in which they went beyond the niceties and superficial dialogue that so often marks such groups, and met each other on a deeper and more profound level. "Life-changing." "Transforming."

171

"Enlightening." "Beyond expectations" were some of the words participants used to describe this study. We hope to go even deeper.

So you can imagine my surprise and deep disappointment when the General Assembly of the Presbyterian Church (USA) this past summer took several actions that not only showed deep insensitivity to our relations with our Jewish brothers and sisters, but also set us back in our understanding of how we as Christians are to view our Jewish friends. It kind of picks the scab off the question of whether the everlasting covenant to Abraham has been superseded…cancelled… by a new covenant, and whether Paul had it wrong in his understanding that Gentiles and Jews are included in that covenant. What we're talking about here is just how comprehensive God's love might be…

The first action had to do with a Presbyterian congregation that has been established in Philadelphia, a so-called Messianic congregation called Avodat Yisrael. According to the General Assembly reports, it is an outreach to unaffiliated Jews, people in interfaith marriages and secularized people of Jewish heritage and invites them to recognize Jesus as the messiah, convert to Christianity, and yet still observe Jewish religious and cultural practices.

If one were to walk into worship at Avodat Yisrael, it would be hard to tell if you were in a synagogue or a church. The Torah, for instance would be reverenced as in Shabbat services when the Torah is taken from the tabernacle. Holidays such as Passover, Yom Kippur and Rosh Hashanah are all observed as are Christmas and Easter.

Now, this is the kind of thing that any number of inter-faith families do in their own homes, with meaningful results. But there is a significant difference between what happens in holy worship and what happens in the home. In Christian worship, for example, not only is the sermon preached and heard, but the sacraments are administered. At Avodat Yisrael communion is administered, but only after a break in the service so that those who might be offended can leave. What does this say about the integrity of our own worship when that which we hold to be sacred is optional?

But more importantly, the underlying theological inference at Avodat Yisrael is that Judaism in and of itself, is not enough. That in order to inherit the promise of the everlasting covenant of salvation, one must convert to Christianity, or to at least some form of Christianity.

That's not the case historically with Presbyterians. In 1987, a watershed document from the General Assembly affirmed that "both the church and the Jewish people are elected by God for witness to the world, and…the relationship of the church to contemporary Jews is based on that gracious and irrevocable election of both." It went on to say that "dialogue is the proper form of witness with Jewish people, since the same scripture that attests to our relationship with God through Jesus Christ also makes clear God's faithfulness to the covenant with the Jewish people."

And yet in spite of our tradition, in spite of some of these underlying assumptions that are offensive to both Jews and many Presbyterians, the General Assembly chose to do something new and different for Presbyterians. They voted to study the issue: to re-examine and strengthen the relationship between Christians and Jews, with particular attention to its implications for Presbyterian evangelism and new church development. I guess we'll have to study what the words "everlasting" and "covenant" mean.

Some of us were hoping for something stronger—a rejection of support for Avodat Yisrael, and a suspension of further funding of messianic new church developments during the study, but it was not to be.

The second issue which went totally under the radar of many of us (Avodat Yisrael had been brewing for over a year), was the authorization of the exploration of a "selective divestment of church funds from those companies whose business in Israel is found to be directly or indirectly causing harm or suffering to innocent people."

Well, this is what really caused a storm, including editorials in the Los Angeles Times and the Wall Street Journal. Much of the information about the process has been distorted or false. Both editorials claimed divestment was a done deed, whereas in reality it was sent to the Mission Responsibility through Investment Committee for study, to report back to the General Assembly Council in March 2005, to work with those companies in the meantime, and then to make a final recommendation to the next General Assembly, which will be in 2006. It is not a done deal.

Still, it was a disturbing vote for many of us. Through the years Presbyterians have sought to be more even-handed on the issue of peacemaking in the Middle East. Dating back over 35 years, the General Assembly has expressed deep concern over the innocent loss of life and the escalating violence on all sides. It has consistently called for mutual security guarantees, for a negotiated, equitable peace, for an end to attacks on innocent people on both sides, and for the United States to be an even handed broker for peace. All of these were re-iterated this year.

But in calling for possible divestment the Assembly has wrongly invited comparisons to the policies it advocated in attempting

174

(successfully) to overthrow apartheid in South Africa. There are several significant and crucial differences: In South Africa, divestment was actually encouraged by the black community there. Desmond Tutu, Allen Boesak, Nelson Mandela and others said that, though it might cause suffering on their part, they were willing to suffer in order to have apartheid reversed. We divested because the situation was so clear, so black and white (if you don't mind the image), that when the oppressed asked us to take action, we did. But we only did so after considerable study, and only as a last resort.

One of the most significant responses to this motion to divest that we really need to pay attention to has been from Jewish groups who have often been critical of Israeli actions on the West Bank and in the building of the wall. Rabbis for Human Rights, a group that has engaged in civil disobedience to prevent Israeli authorities from demolishing Palestinian homes, saw this resolution as a "call for discrimination against Jews." B'nai B'rith, the Jewish fraternal organization and longtime partner in dialogue with Presbyterians, has called publicly for an end to dialogue with the PC (USA).

Violence and injustice are not always one-sided problems and should not be portrayed as such. There have been plenty of victims of war among Palestinians, to be sure. And there have been plenty of victims of war among Israelis. It would seem to me that the church would be far wiser to encourage a peace process in the Middle East, led by the United States, that holds all parties accountable both for past acts of violence and for work towards reconciliation. Now, with the passing of Yassir Arafat, the time could be ripe. It is my prayer that the President seizes this moment.

For there is plenty of suffering to go around. Talk to a Palestinian Christian and hear of the toll the occupation has taken on his life. Talk to an Israeli, who now wonders whenever he sees a pregnant woman with a coat on if that woman is a suicide bomber. Talk to a Palestinian who has to travel two hours to go to her place of work because of the wall. Talk to an Israeli, who knows that she is surrounded on all sides by people who deny her right to exist and whose cruise missiles are only a button away. There is plenty of suffering to go around, and a punitive resolution which is not at all even handed, and in which every avenue of negotiation and discussion has not yet been fully exhausted is not the way to go. The Assembly in both of these actions has seriously damaged in one fell swoop what many of us have spent a lifetime trying to build up.

So why do we even bother with the General Assembly and with resolutions like this? And how should we as Presbyterians at Idlewild relate to our Jewish brothers and sisters?

First, Presbyterians believe that God's will is determined best not by a single individual, like a pope, or a bishop, or a preacher, handing down the definitive divine purpose. Nor is it discovered simply in isolation, reading scripture alone, and searching the depths of one's own heart. Presbyterians believe that God's will is best discerned when a group of people gather and study scripture, pray, debate, listen to each other, and hear the voices of the suffering, study some more and pray some more, and seek the guidance of the Spirit of God. It can be a healthy and creative process, and can actually give guidance to people seeking the wisdom of the church on difficult issues.

The Presbyterian Church has long believed it's important to take stands on public issues of moral concern. In 1954, the Presbyterian Church in the south supported public school desegregation, in 1983, equal rights for women; 1985, divestment in South Africa to help end apartheid; 1995, a ban to end land mines; 1998, reduction of greenhouse gases. Each of these positions were controversial at the time, (and often cost the church something) but in looking back we can be grateful for that public witness, and now these positions are accepted by many if not most Americans. The issue is not whether to speak, but how. I remain sinfully proud to be Presbyterian and remain committed to its processes, but deeply disappointed in these and other actions.

Second, we must understand that God's covenant to Abraham in Genesis 17, renewed to Isaac and Jacob, remembered by David , echoed by Isaiah and Jeremiah , and passed down to all generations is an everlasting covenant. God has promised to honor that covenant, so we shall also. For all of the lumps that Paul takes these days (some of them deservedly so) the one issue that dominated his writings, indeed his major contribution to the cause of Christianity, was the universality of God's love. "Gentiles share the inheritance with the Jews," he wrote in Ephesians… "fellow heirs" of the covenant is the way the King James Version puts it, "partakers of the same promise."

He talked about a secret, a mystery that he had been given to share, and it was that the love and the mercy and the grace of God were not just meant for one small group, but for the whole of humanity. And the tragedy, the overriding sin of religious people (first the Jews that Paul was addressing, and later the Christians) is the way in which this inclusive character of God's love has come to be construed as something very exclusive. I don't know if there is a greater crime against God than the way in which we have taken something comprehensive—embracing—reconciling—and turned it into an instrument of divisiveness. Moreover, to market God's love on the basis of its exclusiveness is a crime beyond compare.

I imagine that when God wakes up in the morning and thinks about all that is going on in the world God created….Iraq, the Sudan,

177

Israel, Palestine, Afghanistan, North Korea, Russia, Washington, Memphis, and then begins to fashion the agenda for the day to those things that worry God the most, I imagine that the so-called conversion of the Jews is nowhere to be found. God's agenda is the mending of the created order. God's agenda, God's dream, is the wholeness, the shalom of the human family. And God's agenda should be our agenda. The covenant is an everlasting covenant to all generations.

Third, as we reflect upon our relationship with our Jewish brothers and sisters, we as Christians need to be in touch with our own Jewishness. Jesus was a Jew. His parents were Jewish. His bible, his worship, his prayers were Jewish. His philosophical orientation, his theological perspective were all shaped by his Jewishness. Moreover, every Old Testament writer and every New Testament writer (except Luke) was Jewish.

Why is this so important? Think of how Germany in the 1930's might have been different had the church remembered its own Jewishness. Or how the south might have been different as well in the way Christians treated Jews and blacks had we taken the Hebrew Scriptures more seriously. Rather, the church believed, like many evangelical Christians today, that the Old Testament was seen exclusively as law and the New Testament solely as grace; that the God of the Old Testament was judgmental; the God of the New Testament was loving. The Old Testament was plundered for a few devotional passages and a few verses which validated the messianic credentials of Jesus, but the larger treasure was ignored. As a church in the south we concentrated on private piety and personal salvation to the degree that we lost all sense of the legitimate calling of the law—to do justice, to love mercy, and to walk humbly with the Almighty through the streets of the city and the councils of the nations. That would not have happened if we remembered our Jewishness.

I still remember the pain in a young man's voice when he described to me recently what it was like to grow up here in Memphis and not be able to join a club that his best friends joined because one of his parents was Jewish.

And finally, as we continue to engage in dialogue with our Jewish friends, we might do so with what Jonathan Sacks, the chief rabbi in England has called "the dignity of difference," finding in the human "thou" a fragment of the Divine "Thou," the voice of wisdom from others telling us something we need to know. It is vital if we are to survive in a new world.

Well, this is not the first time the Assembly has acted ill advisedly, nor will it be the last. But it is my prayer that Idlewild might continue to be a place of hospitality where Jew and Gentile alike may seek after God with humility, earnestness of purpose, and openness of heart. We do this as we look to honor the great head of the church, our Jewish brother Jesus, whom we know as God's child and as our savior. In his spirit and in his name, we dare not ignore the deep soil of our Jewish roots. And in that soil we celebrate the one faith by which the common covenant is given, that we shall be God's people, and that that covenant shall be an everlasting covenant to all generations...everlasting to all generations.

The Touch

March 6, 2011
(Transfiguration Sunday)

Matthew 17:1-9

Six days later, Jesus took with him Peter and James and his brother John and led them up a high mountain, by themselves. 2And he was transfigured before them, and his face shone like the sun, and his clothes became dazzling white. 3Suddenly there appeared to them Moses and Elijah, talking with him. 4Then Peter said to Jesus, "Lord, it is good for us to be here; if you wish, I will make three dwellings here, one for you, one for Moses, and one for Elijah." 5While he was still speaking, suddenly a bright cloud overshadowed them, and from the cloud a voice said, "This is my Son, the Beloved; with him I am well pleased; listen to him!" 6When the disciples heard this, they fell to the ground and were overcome by fear. 7But Jesus came and touched them, saying, "Get up and do not be afraid." 8And when they looked up, they saw no one except Jesus himself alone. 9As they were coming down the mountain, Jesus ordered them, "Tell no one about the vision until after the Son of Man has been raised from the dead."

Prayer: Dear God, we thank you for this time together, and grateful for this time of silence and stillness. Speak to us today. Come to us in word and sacrament. Startle us once again with your love, in Jesus Christ our Lord. Amen.

LAST WEEK MARGARET SHARED WITH YOU a little occupational secret: that even pastors with great faith have worries and anxieties. Allow me to let you in on another one: Sometimes people want to talk to you about God when you do not necessarily want to talk to them about God.

Here's a nightmare: I'm up in an airplane, thousands of feet above ground, nowhere to escape, and the person next to me discovers I am a minister. "So tell me," He says, "why should I believe in God?" But there is the other option, just as bad. The person next to me has just come back from an evangelistic crusade, sitting there with a great big Bible in her lap, and she wants to know if I have been really, truly, born again. And when. And where.

Those haven't happened to me, but awhile back I was at a sit down dinner. An elegant affair. I knew one of the people next to me, but didn't know the other. We were making small talk, the weather, sports, even a little politics, and as the salad plates are taken away and the entrees served, the man to my left said "Do you mind if I change the subject?"

"Not at all," I said.

"Well, good, because just recently I have been thinking that it makes no sense to believe in a personal God." Suddenly the salmon and rice pilaf didn't look quite as appetizing. "You see, Steve … your name is Steve, isn't it? … I accept the idea that there probably was a force behind the force that set off the big bang, but the idea of God having characteristics like a merciful heart, or God's becoming involved in human affairs … does that really make sense?"

To be honest, that actually led to a remarkably mutually respectful conversation. He talked about what he believed about God. I talked about what I believe about God. And after that I thought about how important it is for the church and for its ministers, wherever we are, to be genuinely respectful of the real questions that people are asking about God and what God has to do with us and our world. I think that the church and its ministers make a mistake when we assume that every-body has the answers to the basic theological questions already figured out. The basic ones — Is there a God? Is God for or against us? Is God far away or near? Who is Jesus Christ? People struggle with these questions. Pastors sometimes struggle with these questions. Whoever asks these deserve to have their questions taken seriously.

After all, we say we are "disciples of Jesus Christ." Did you know that the word "disciple" simply means "learner," or "one who is learning?" To be a disciple of Christ is to be someone who is learning, or wants to learn, who Jesus was and who he is for us and for our world today.

The central claim of the Christian faith is that in Jesus Christ God came near. Christ's giving of himself away for others was nothing less than God's giving God's own self away, surrendering to the forces of death, so that everlasting, abundant new life could be released upon the world.

Now that's a mouthful, and if you didn't get it all, don't feel bad about it. I don't always fully understand it all myself. And here's something that comforts me: the original disciples, those who knew him the best, didn't understand it either. They had a hard time comprehending that the great God who had created the heavens and the earth had chosen to live on earth with us. It was really only after he died and had been raised from the dead and felt his presence with them that they "got it."

So one day shortly after he had befuddled them by talking about how he was going to suffer and be killed, and rise again, and telling them to take up a cross and follow him, he felt he just needed to take some of them away and show them who he was and what was what. Matthew crisply and dramatically describes what happens: "Jesus led three of the disciples up a high mountain, and there he was transfigured before them. His face shone like the sun, and his clothes became dazzling white. Suddenly, Moses and Elijah appeared, signifying the fulfillment of the law and the prophets. Then suddenly, a bright cloud overshadowed them and from the cloud a voice spoke saying, 'This is my Son, the Beloved ... listen to what he has to say.'"

Here, more than anywhere else in his life, it became clear to his disciples: This is the one who made clear the true and essential nature of God.

I like the way Marcus Borg puts it: "Jesus discloses that at the center of everything is a reality that is in love with us, and who wills our well-being." Borg takes one more step: "Jesus counters the conventional wisdom's understanding of God as one who make demands on us and before whom we must cower and fear." Here is a compassionate God who wants to be close to us; who is the force of the transformation of all of human life.

I didn't get into all of that at the dinner with the nice man. But I also realized then and now that I could never prove to him or to you or to anyone that at the center of things there is a reality that loves us and wishes us well. All I can say is that through the grace of God we can come to trust that God is real. That God is close. That God's wish for us is that we grow in faith and hope and love.

You can't argue a person into belief. I quit trying long ago. I wish my words could make it happen. I wish we could convince one another that God is real, was enfleshed in Jesus Christ. Theologian Dorothy Soelle speaks for me in her book *Theology for Skeptics* when she writes: "To speak about God — that is what I would like to do and where I always fail." We come to know God and under-stand God not by proof or argument. We come to know God because God wishes to be known, as was so obvious that shining day on the Mount of Transfiguration.

You know, this text comes up every year the Sunday before Lent, which means I have preached on it around 30 years. But there is always something new. Anna Carter Florence, professor of preaching at Columbia Theological Seminary, walked through this passage with the officers this past January, asking us to pay attention to the verbs. "The verbs tell us who God is, and tell us who we are."

And so I did. The divine voice spoke, and the disciples "fall on their faces, overcome by fear." That's us, isn't it? Fear. It's what drives so much of our lives, so many of our decisions. Those verbs tell us who we are. They are paralyzed. They cannot move or think. But here is what I have always missed: "And Jesus came and touched them, and said "Get up and do not be afraid." The voice, the cloud, the mystery, the majesty all boldly broadcasting that is was Almighty God they were dealing with, and Jesus walked over to them and touched them. The God who created the heavens and the earth was willing to come among us and touch us in the place of our deepest need.

"Is there anything that banishes human fear better than a simple human touch?" For John Calvin, this was God's great genius. He wrote "In Christ, God made himself little in order to accommodate himself to our capacity."

That's a long way from the distant, big-bang God isn't it, to the thought of God's eternal hand reaching out to touch our very human shoulders, so that we may know we are not alone?

Some of you might know the story that the surgeon/writer Richard Selzer described as he witnessed a remarkable sight one day in his work at a hospital. He writes:

"I stand by the bed where a young woman lies, her face postoperative, her mouth twisted in palsy, clownish. A tiny twig of the facial nerve, the one to the muscles of her mouth, has been severed…to remove the tumor in her cheek, I had cut the little nerve.

The young husband is in the room. He stands on the opposite side of the bed, and together they seem to dwell in the evening lamplight, isolated from me, private….

"Will my mouth always be like this?" she asks.

"Yes," I say, "it will. It is because the nerve was cut."

She nods and is silent. But the young man smiles. "I like it," he says, "It is kind of cute."

He bends to kiss her crooked mouth. I am so close I can see how he twists his own lips to accommodate her, to show her that their kiss still works … I hold my breath and let the wonder in."

Don't get bogged down in the details of what actually happened that day on the mountain. Simply think of it as God's bending over to our brokenness, to our need, to our loneliness, to our fear, and saying in love, "Don't worry. No matter what your brokenness, no matter how lost you feel, I love you."

Amen.

Passages I Love To Hate: "To Lie with a Male as With a Woman"

July 31, 2001

Preached in a summer Sermon Series on "Passages I Love to Hate")

Leviticus 18:19-30; Acts 8:26-40

19 You shall not approach a woman to uncover her nakedness while she is in her menstrual uncleanness. 20 You shall not have sexual relations with your kinsman's wife, and defile yourself with her. 21 You shall not give any of your offspring to sacrifice them to Moloch, and so profane the name of your God: I am the Lord. 22 You shall not lie with a male as with a woman; it is an abomination. 23 You shall not have sexual relations with any animal and defile yourself with it, nor shall any woman give herself to an animal to have sexual relations with it: it is perversion. 24 Do not defile yourselves in any of these ways, for by all these practices the nations I am casting out before you have defiled themselves. 25 Thus the land became defiled; and I punished it for its iniquity, and the land vomited out its inhabitants. 26 But you shall keep my statutes and my ordinances and commit none of these abominations, either the citizen or the alien who resides among you 27 (for the inhabitants of the land, who were before you, committed all of these abominations, and the land became defiled); 28 otherwise the land will vomit you out for defiling it, as it vomited out the nation that was before you. 29 For whoever commits any of these abominations shall be cut off from their people. 30 So keep my charge not to commit any of these

*abominations that were done before you, and not to defile yourselves by them: I
am the Lord your God.*

Acts 8: 26-40

*26 Then an angel of the Lord said to Philip, "Get up and go toward the south
to the road that goes down from Jerusalem to Gaza." (This is a wilderness road.)
27 So he got up and went. Now there was an Ethiopian eunuch, a court official
of the Candace, queen of the Ethiopians, in charge of her entire treasury. He had
come to Jerusalem to worship 28 and was returning home; seated in his chariot,
he was reading the prophet Isaiah. 29 Then the Spirit said to Philip, "Go over
to this chariot and join it." 30 So Philip ran up to it and heard him reading the
prophet Isaiah. He asked, "Do you understand what you are reading?" 31 He
replied, "How can I, unless someone guides me?" And he invited Philip to get in
and sit beside him. 32 Now the passage of the scripture that he was reading was
this: "Like a sheep he was led to the slaughter, and like a lamb silent before its
shearer, so he does not open his mouth. 33 In his humiliation justice was denied
him. Who can describe his generation? For his life is taken away from the earth."
34 The eunuch asked Philip, "About whom, may I ask you, does the prophet
say this, about himself or about someone else?" 35 Then Philip began to speak,
and starting with this scripture, he proclaimed to him the good news about Jesus.
36 As they were going along the road, they came to some water; and the eunuch
said, "Look, here is water! What is to prevent me from being baptized?" 37 38
He commanded the chariot to stop, and both of them, Philip and the eunuch,
went down into the water, and Philip baptized him. 39 When they came up out
of the water, the Spirit of the Lord snatched Philip away; the eunuch saw him
no more, and went on his way rejoicing. 40 But Philip found himself at Azotus,
and as he was passing through the region, he proclaimed the good news to all the
towns until he came to Caesarea.*

Prayer: Bless us, O God, with a reverent sense of your presence, that your Holy Spirit might comfort, discomfort, or even startle us with the truth of your unbounded love in Jesus Christ. And may words of my mouth and the meditations of our hearts be found acceptable in thy sight, O Lord, our strength and our redeemer. Amen.

SOME SERMONS CAN BE VERY DOGMATIC when the word of the Lord is very clear and it is easy to declare "Thus saith the Lord." This sermon is not one of those. Nor is it offered with a "This is what you should think" admonition. There is no more essential doctrine in our Reformed Presbyterian tradition than the belief that God alone is Lord of the conscience. So I offer this sermon more as an invitation to talk, to listen, to learn, to pray, to study as we seek God's will together in the struggle to be faithful to the God of justice and mercy embodied in the person of Jesus Christ, and attested to in holy scripture.

I do so with the realization that this is a divisive issue for the church, and not just Idlewild and not just the Presbyterian Church (USA). Some have said that this is the most schismatic issue for the church since slavery and abolition in the 19th century. It has become so divisive that in many corners of the church it has become impossible even to talk about, to engage in civil dialogue, in moral discourse. Yet to ignore it is to violate the mandate of the gospel which affirms that no corner of life is excluded from Christian concern — especially not those having to do with human relationships. And the church, whose foundation is Jesus Christ and the oneness we have in him, ought to be the one place where we can talk about it in a thoughtful, non-emotive way. I hope this sermon sheds more light than heat.

Finally, for those of you who are visiting here or are newcomers to the church, I want you to know that I have preached around 400 sermons here over the past 11 years (no wonder we have air conditioning problems ... that's a lot of hot air!), but this is the first time I have ever explicitly addressed these difficult passages and issues from the pulpit. Our purpose is to glorify God and enjoy God, to preach Christ and Christ crucified, and to call all of us to faithful obedience to our baptismal vows in every corner of our lives. This text from Leviticus is a passage I love to hate, and we are better off going through it and not around it because the implications of avoiding it can be deadly.

So let me read to you excerpts from a letter I received from a former parishioner when I left Atlanta and came here to Idlewild. I have her permission to use it, though I have changed the names:

Dear Steve,

I want to thank you for helping Wanda and me find a church home where we felt accepted as a family. As a P.K., church was naturally a big part of my life growing up. Unfortunately, I didn't always see the better sides of people in the church. I actually saw more negatives than positives, and so when I became an adult, I set aside the church. Over 20 years passed before I was able to begin again exploring my spiritual side, so that healing from my past could begin.

Wanda and I originally visited your church because we were looking for some place for her to take her son that was not as anti-tolerant as the churches his dad regularly took him to. I asked a friend what church was most likely, and she suggested my old stomping grounds, the Presbyterian Church (USA) and yours in particular.

189

So this letter is about faith. Faith in the future, that God has a master plan that will work out to our benefit. Faith that the church will see Wanda and me, and her son, Sam, as a family, not an abomination

This letter is about hope. Hope that the church will someday allow full inclusion into the life of the church for Wanda, for me, and for our family.

Most of all, this letter is about love. The unconditional love that God has for us. Our rather feeble, frequently misguided, and often misinterpreted attempts to emulate that unconditional love towards our fellow human beings. And finally, the love of God and humanity that shows in everything you do.

Now I read that letter because it illustrates for me better than any words I can say, that any consideration of these texts about homosexuality must be conducted in the context of the personal and not just the theoretical. Homosexuality is not preeminently an issue. It is preeminently people. As God does not deal with us abstractly and impersonally, rather as individuals — as one who numbers the hairs on our heads, who hears the beat of our hearts, every splash of our tears, who calls us by name … so we who are God's must seek in all our strivings to deal with one another in such a fashion. We are talking about people.

Furthermore, we are not just dealing with people "out there." We are talking about our brothers and our sisters and our sons and our daughters and aunts and uncles, and we are talking about our sisters and brothers in Christ like Wanda and Joyce, whose letter I read, whom we have baptized, and with whom we share Christian fellowship and break bread in the Christian community.

And so we turn to scripture for guidance. That sounds easy, doesn't it? And for some it is easy. Take the five or six verses in a cursory reading of the entire Bible that seem to speak to homosexuality and one could conclude that it condemns homosexuality unequivocally. End of discussion. But it is a mistake to look to the Bible to close a discussion; the Bible seeks to open one.

You see, the Bible is violated whenever it is used as a catalogue of proof texts to support my own prejudice. Everybody knows, I assume, that there are passages of scripture which can be, and often have been, used in support of slavery, of brutal war, of women keeping their heads covered and their mouths shut in church. Now, it is no more legitimate to pick and choose those passages of scripture which seem to point to an anti-homosexual bias than it is to pick and choose those passages which seem to support an anti-woman or pro-slavery bias.

What we need to remember is that the revelation of God is in the person of Jesus Christ. It is a revelation which, to be sure, comes to us through the Scriptures which mirror also the cultural mores and biases of their day. (Paul's teaching that women should keep their heads covered in church, for example.) Therefore, any proper interpretation of Scripture needs to take its cues, not from isolated passages here and there, but from the total revelation of Jesus' life — teaching, death, and resurrection…the life study of which, incidentally, reveals not a word about homosexuality. The fact is, Jesus simply never mentioned it.

What we do have are some problematic texts in Leviticus. "You shall not lie with a male as a woman; it is an abomination." (Lev. 18:22) There is another text that calls for the death penalty for anyone who breaks that admonition. That seems clear, doesn't it? But in that same code, called "the Holiness Code," we find instructions about

191

what times of the month are appropriate and what times of the month are inappropriate for sexual relations. In the same code, those who curse their parents shall be stoned to death. (Lev. 20:9, Deut. 21:18-21. There are prohibitions against wearing clothes made of two different materials (I plead guilty!) and against shaving (I'd be safe there!). Others who are condemned are those who are blind or lame, or those with a broken foot or hand, or a man with a blemish in his eyes (Lev. 21:18-20). These and many other actions are condemned because they defy purity and weaken the cultural identification of the people of Israel in the Promised Land. So great was the principle of ritual and ethnic purity that to violate it was in most cases to warrant the sentence of death.

We need to understand the context that led to the Holiness Code (the need to set themselves apart, to be pure, to procreate), but we also need to understand that we are no longer bound by the rules of the code. Both Jesus and Paul found the details of ritual purity irrelevant. They were both concerned with the purity of heart.

The other Old Testament passage often used in discussions of homosexuality is the Sodom and Gomorrah story in Genesis 19. I won't go into the whole gory story, except to say that when we interpret a story such as this one, we need first of all to see how it was interpreted in scripture, not how the church interprets it now, because it is at least possible that the church has imposed its own bias. That's especially true in how the church has historically treated women.

Whenever the story of the destruction of Sodom and Gomorrah is referred to in the Bible, the sin of homosexuality is never mentioned. When Ezekiel or Isaiah or Jesus mention the sin of Sodom, they allude to the sin of pride, idleness, neglect of the poor; Jesus referred

192

to the sin of inhospitality. It was a wicked place, but nowhere does the Bible state that homosexuality was the wickedness in question.

As we turn to the New Testament, we find Paul writing in Romans (1:26ff) of "dishonorable passions" and natural and unnatural relations, and it is clear that throughout the history of the interpretation of those passages, the assumption has been that he is referring to homosexual relationships. Recent scholarship has suggested that Paul, who assumed the heterosexuality of all persons, is not talking about homosexuality as an orientation, but only about male prostitution and pedophilia, which were a part of the culture of heterosexuality in both Rome and Corinth, and it is in the context of idolatry.

These same scholars do a lot of word studies and sociological studies of the ancient near east and come to similar conclusions about the two other New Testament passages traditionally associated with homosexuality, I Timothy 2 and I Corinthians 5. A very careful reading of the Greek in the Timothy text shows that what is being condemned is a very specific form of pederasty in which young boys were enslaved for sexual purposes, and one can hardly argue with the evil it represents.

These are difficult hermeneutical problems, stemming from the fact that the contemporary church is asking the Scripture questions the culture in which the Scriptures were written did not ask. There is no doubt that Paul condemned pederasty, and male prostitution, those same sex relationships in which there is oppression or power exerted against the will of another human being. But what is patently unknown to Paul and to the ancient world of the Bible was the concept of orientation, mutual same-sex relationships in which there are expressions of constancy, faithfulness, trust, and commitment.

193

That's it. Those are the references in scripture to homosexuality. So where does that leave us? Certainly, at the very least we can say that we need a higher order of Christian ethics than proof-texting provides; that is, taking one verse out of context and making it gospel. It is an issue that will be best served, not by pointing to Levitical laws buried deep in the back of the Bible, but in looking at the bigger picture of the ways of how God relates with human beings. God rarely, if ever, contentedly pats the community of faith on the back and says, "You're absolutely right to keep things pure, exclude those people. My grace was just for you and for people like you and not for those other people." The picture the Bible gives us of God is a picture of God who is always having to go around grabbing the faith community by the neck and prodding it, sometimes kicking and screaming, toward a new understanding of the essential inclusiveness of divine grace.

That's the story of the early church in Acts. Notice how the Holy Spirit continually broadens that community's understanding of how wide and deep God's love extends. There were 11 frightened apostles, they added one to the mix. Then at Pentecost the Spirit included Jews from all over the known world, Parthians, Medes, Elamites and the rest. And then in today's story you have Philip traveling in the desert taking the gospel to the (gasp!) Samaritans and he met up with an Ethiopian eunuch from Queen Candace's court.

Now the Torah, the Jewish law, forbade eunuchs from even entering the assembly of the Lord. (Deut. 23:1) because of their sexual difference. This man happened to be reading the prophet Isaiah. Philip explained to him that the person Isaiah was talking about was Jesus Christ, and this good news moved him to the core.

They come up on some water. Now, remember, this is in the desert. There is no water in the desert. Luke, who wrote this, felt this was a

194

"God-thing." And the eunuch asked Philip "What is to prevent me from being baptized?" It's an interesting way to phrase the question, but yes, there was something. The law. The fact that he was sexually unfit.

But Philip was shaped more by the Spirit than by the law; more by the love of Jesus Christ than the legalism of Moses. And Philip baptized the eunuch and the eunuch went on his way rejoicing. And then just a few chapters later Peter has a vision, a dream that leads him to sit down and eat with a (double gasp!) Gentile, which the law clearly forbade. But not the Holy Spirit. Peter concluded: "Truly I perceive that God shows no partiality, but in every nation anyone who fears God and does what is right is acceptable to God" You and I are here today because those early church leaders were not bound by the old interpretations of the law, but were open to a new thing God's Spirit was doing because of the revelation in Jesus Christ.

So let me conclude by making some suggestions about how we might direct our discussions and thoughts and hearts as we reclaim our own baptism and struggle to be faithful, especially in light of the changes our denomination has made in more inclusive, but in some ways more strict, ordination standards.

I've already made the first suggestion, and that is to pay attention to the broad and sweeping movement of the Bible which describes a direction for the creation that God has set in motion. And I see from Genesis 1 to Revelation 22 the shaping and forming of a God who creates the world, loves it, and who reconciles, sacrifices, and covenants with the earth and its people, moving us toward a unity and peace that we have not fully achieved. The watershed event, of course, in the unfolding story of God's creative work among us was Jesus Christ, God's limitless expression of love and sacrifice given to us as a gift given to draw all people to himself.

Let's not get hung up on things that are not central to that gospel. Rather, may we be open to the Spirit's leading us to a more loving and merciful interpretation. We do that with a certain amount of humility, because we always have to be open to the possibility that we might be wrong. The church has been wrong in the past about many things. And it was not a rejection of scripture when the church finally took a decisive stand against slavery. It was an affirmation of the mind of Christ doing a new thing in our midst. The church was wrong for 2,000 years about the role of women, and when we finally attained a new understanding about the gifts of women for leadership in the church, we were not denying the authority of scripture. We believe that Jesus Christ was doing a new thing in our midst. You never know!

The second suggestion would be to listen, I mean really listen, to each other, especially with people who are different. As I have said before, one of the greatest gifts Idlewild has is our wide diversity of opinions, experiences, theologies and interpretations. That's how I grow spiritually. And I have done a lot of listening over the past few months. Here is what I have heard:

•I have heard, without exception, a sincere desire, to live into the vision that we believe God has given us, that Idlewild be a community in which all who enter might find a home. We may differ on strategies, but there has been unanimity about us being a church that welcomes all. Without exception — young, old, new member, longtime member — there has not been one person that I have heard who has objected to that vision. I thank God for that, and for you.

•I have heard a lot of fear expressed — fear over the unknown, fear over lessening the authority of scripture, fear about losing members if we open our doors more widely, fear about the effects controversial issues such as this might have on giving, and active participation. Fear about what our friends in other churches might think. And I have some of those fears as well. We need to listen to those who voice their concerns, and to be attentive to our own fears. And what I have found when I have examined my own fears, my greatest fear is not being faithful to Jesus Christ, my Lord and Savior.

•I have heard of another fear that I needed to hear. This highlights the importance of listening to others who might be different from us — this was the fear that gays often have when they enter a church for the first time. I have learned that it is terribly hard and scary. Will I be accepted? Will I get the Bible thrown at me? Will they see me as an abomination? If I bring my child to be baptized, will they baptize her? It took Joyce 20 years to enter a church after some bad experiences. It's a whole different set of fears that long-time members might have. But they are fears and need to be listened to every bit as much as the fears I expressed earlier.

A third suggestion would be that we not only listen to each other, but our reformed tradition reminds us that God also speaks to us through disciplines other than the purely theological, which is to say, we need to listen to the expertise from other professions. Is homosexuality an illness? Nearly forty years ago the American Psychiatric Association removed homosexuality from its list of mental disorders. Is it a choice? The most persuasive data that comes from the scientific community is that gays and lesbians appear to have no more choice as to their sexual orientation than to most heterosexual people. What that means to me is that the God we know in Jesus Christ would hardly bring one into being, if God did not also intend that person's worth to be guaranteed and held in sacred trust in the world in which God made.

197

The final suggestion is that there should be a single, ethical standard for all people: gays and straights, men and women, married and single. Any infidelity on the part of anybody, be they homosexual or heterosexual, is not in line with the Christian gospel. The abuse of one's sexuality, the idolatry of sex, promiscuity, using other people for the sole purpose of sexual gratification, whether a person is gay or straight, I hope we are all in agreement that that is clearly wrong, and those kinds of behavior are sinful. Put more positively, the single standard for all relationships should be based upon mutuality, commitment, constancy, trust, and love.

That's what I have to offer about these difficult passages I love to hate. As I said at the beginning, the consequences of not taking them seriously and through the lens of Jesus Christ can be deadly. At least one-third of all teenage suicides are due to their struggles with sexuality, and fears of rejection by family, friends, and church, and bullying.

I have to be open to the possibility that I might be wrong. I don't think I am, but I might be, because the church has been wrong about plenty of issues through the years, and therefore what it boils down to for me is that in my search for more understanding and answers to these difficult questions — if I err, I am going to err on the side of acceptance, not condemnation; if I err, I am going to err on the side of compassion, not doctrine; I am going to err on the side of grace, and not law. For that unconditional grace is what the Scripture means when it says we are to love one another ... even as God has loved us.

I hope I have been faithful to my Lord and Savior, and our foundation as a church, Jesus Christ.

Amen.

What If?

(Martin Luther King, Jr. Weekend)

I Samuel 3:1-10, John 1:43-51

Now the boy Samuel was ministering to the Lord under Eli. The word of the Lord was rare in those days; visions were not widespread. 2At that time Eli, whose eyesight had begun to grow dim so that he could not see, was lying down in his room; 3the lamp of God had not yet gone out, and Samuel was lying down in the temple of the Lord, where the ark of God was. 4Then the Lord called, "Samuel! Samuel!" and he said, "Here I am!" 5and ran to Eli, and said, "Here I am, for you called me." But he said, "I did not call; lie down again." So he went and lay down. 6The Lord called again, "Samuel!" Samuel got up and went to Eli, and said, "Here I am, for you called me." But he said, "I did not call, my son; lie down again." 7Now Samuel did not yet know the Lord, and the word of the Lord had not yet been revealed to him. 8The Lord called Samuel again, a third time. And he got up and went to Eli, and said, "Here I am, for you called me." Then Eli perceived that the Lord was calling the boy. 9Therefore Eli said to Samuel, "Go, lie down; and if he calls you, you shall say, 'Speak, Lord, for your servant is listening.'" So Samuel went and lay down in his place. 10Now the Lord came and stood there, calling as before, "Samuel! Samuel!" And Samuel said, "Speak, for your servant is listening."

Prayer: O God of the ages, God of today, God of tomorrow, as we hear your word today, silence all of the other voices that surround us, voices clamoring for our attention, so that we might be startled enough to hear the living word, enabling us to leave from here a bit more loving, a bit more hopeful, a bit more willing to be guided by your Son, Jesus Christ. Amen.

SOME OF YOU MIGHT RECOGNIZE THE Shel Silverstein poem "What-ifs:"

Last night while i lay thinking here

Some what ifs crawled inside my ear.
And pranced and partied all night long
And sang their same old what if song.
What if I'm dumb in school?
What if they've closed the swimming pool?
What if i get beat up?
What if there's poison in my cup?
What if i get sick and die?
What if i flunk the test?
What if green hair grows on my chest?
What if i tear my pants?
What if i never learn to dance?
Everything seems swell and then
The night time what ifs strike again ... The what ifs.

Of course, adults play what-if too, especially when they reach a certain age. Often late at night or all alone they will drag out some old class yearbook, browse through the pages and pages of pictures of classmates they knew best, and recall those days when they first knew them in school (10, 20, 30 or more years ago.) Inevitably the eye will halt on certain ones while the mind races back in time, calling up the crazy antics, the fun, the excitement, the heartbreaks. But also the dreams, the ambitions, all those things once talked about doing and becoming after graduation…after we'd grown up.

And then, just as inevitably, they think about those same classmates today. What they have actually done with their lives after graduation—after they have grown up—where they are and who they are today. And that's when the "what-ifs" begin to crawl inside the ear. What if Liz had just not married so early? Of if she had played the field a little more? What if Freddie had taken his studies more seriously and hadn't begun to run with that crowd?

And of course, before long the scenarios shifts to the self...What if I...had gone to the University of Alabama instead of the College of Wooster...had majored in geology instead of history...gone to Vietnam instead of New Haven? "What if...." The What-ifs belong not only to the young.

The two bible stories the lectionary serves up today are scattered with what-ifs-- true to life stories of people who heard---or thought they heard—the voice of God.

First, there's Samuel. Bless his heart, as we say, a shy little kid brought up since the age of two in the Temple under the tutelage of the old and half-blind priest Eli (and that wasn't Samuel's idea, but because his mother Hannah thought she could not have children, and then when little Samuel came along and surprised them all, she interpreted it as God's special gift, and so she gave the child to the service of the Lord in the temple.)

So he was there not with any burning zeal to be there, (he might have looked out the window and seen his friends playing baseball) for though every day he performed his simple duties well, the story indicates that "Samuel did not know the Lord." Hmmm. You would think that after all of that churchy stuff that must have gone on in the temple, after all the temple classes, the youth group trips, the confirmation training, you would think that Samuel would know something about God. You would think that he could say glowing things about his faith, about the community, about the God whom he worships. But he did not know the Lord. How can you live in the temple your whole life and not know the Lord?

Maybe Samuel had had enough and seen enough of his religious family of faith. Maybe you can only take so much of it before it starts to wear on you; we might call it burn out; when your youthful excitement turns to disillusion. He saw the behind the scenes things—some of the ugly, selfish, annoying things that nobody really wants to see in their own faith community. He has seen the hypocrisy, in, for example, the preacher's kids...Eli's sons. They were stealing money from the offering plates, and sleeping around with parishoners right outside the temple gates. No wonder Samuel doesn't know the Lord. He begins to wonder if God still lives in the place. And no wonder the story tells us that "The word of the Lord was rare in those days, there was not a frequent vision."

Maybe Samuel was ready to get out of this place, to jump ship while he still could, while he was still young and bold enough to drive himself out of deep-worn ruts of repetition. But it's God who doesn't let Samuel make that decision. God calls him by name....three times God speaks to this kid who already has one foot out the door, who's got issues with the faith community, the kids who's got questions and struggles with the institution of his faith.

Hear this: God's way of dealing with the brokenness of the house of God is to call the kid who doesn't have everything all figured out; the kid who's got questions and struggles with the institution of his faith.

In the New Testament, the story is a bit different. This time all the players are adults—grown and graduated and already going on profitable career in the fishing business—when they encounter Jesus. After spending some time with him, they decide to change directions....quit the fishing business in favor of a more philosophical, or spiritual quest, becoming as the text puts it in another gospel, "Fishers of people."

Now, it's clear at this point that the disciples are not clear. Somewhat like little Samuel, they are not sure what they have heard, or what it means. But there is sufficient interest, or curiosity, or compulsion; there is something in them that compels them to respond to Jesus' urging "Follow me." "Come and see."

Just imagine all the what-ifs at play here. Late at night and sleep won't come, or maybe in the early dawn when day has not quite broken and the night is hanging on, and the mind is most susceptible. Don't you know Samuel had his moments of wrestling with the What-ifs? "What if...what if what I took for the voice of God was no more than an adolescent insecurity?" And those disciples: There was Simon and Andrew, then Philip and Nathaniel. It all happened so quickly. Don't you imagine there were days of second thoughts and nights of "what-ifs?" wondering if one had acted wisely. Or possibly over-reacted. And wondering—if one had to do it all over again—would one do the same thing? What if?

All of which raises the question "How does God get through? If God wants to get through to you and me, how does God get through?

And if God speaks to some, why doesn't God speak to all? And if God speaks to all, why doesn't God speak as clearly and as convincingly as God does to others?

What if...the voice of God can be explained away as my own craving for love and acceptance?

What if...the voice of God is no more than the subjective whisperings of my own desires?

Or, on the other hand, what if God is all those things God is supposed to be—truth, hope, virtue, love, purpose—How does God get through to folk like us who crave truth, hope, virtue, love, purpose?

Well, I do not know, and scripture does not give us all the answers. But scripture and history give us a few clues, so that we do know some things.

We know, for example, God never speaks to me at the detriment of another. To the grave disappointment of some, I am sure, God does not play favorites and if what I hear is a voice that suggests violence or injustice or exclusiveness toward another person or race or tribe or nation, I know that it is not the voice of the Lord.

We know, for example, the voice of God is always a summons to wholeness—healing, harmony, reconciliation, salvation. It is not the will of God that any be lost, or that any be ill, or that any be less than whole. And any voice that suggests otherwise is clearly not a calling of the Lord. We know that.

We know, for example, that we have to be very careful when evaluating voices because there are so many impersonations out there, so we must be careful not to evaluate by our standards, but by God's. Billy Graham was right on target a few years ago before he became incapacitated when he warned against those televangelists who preach a false gospel of affluence. "They are doing damage to the kingdom of God," he said. And he's right, for God does not call some to affluence at the expense of others. God has a higher standard of values, a clearer set of ethics than that. And we know that.

And we know, from scripture and from human experience, that God often takes the broken, the doubting, the questioning, and the person who doesn't have everything figured out to speak through.

There was the son of a Baptist preacher, who at the age of 13 shocked his Sunday School class and teacher by denying the bodily resurrection of Jesus. That didn't go over so well in that fundamentalist church. Mike, as they called him then, reported later that after that "doubts began to spring forth unrelentingly" in to his college years when he said "he regretted going to church." He had become a skeptic, moving so far away from the religion of his parents, that when a friend later heard that he had become a preacher, "his first reaction was to laugh out loud in disbelief."

That preacher that God called was a kid named Martin Luther King, Jr. He went on to train to be a scholar, had worked on his Ph.D. and was ready for the calm, warm life of academia. But there weren't any jobs available. A church from Montgomery, Alabama wanted to call him as their pastor. "What if….God is calling me to turn in a new direction?" What if….?

And there were more "what-ifs" during his life. What if…. God is calling all people to live together and work together and play together in harmony? What if?

You young people: What if God is calling you to speak out when you see someone being bullied of made fun of because he just doesn't fit in, or because she doesn't wear the right clothes. What if?

Or you adults: What if God is calling you to protest proposed legislation in Tennessee that would make bullying legal, if it were based on religious principles?

One of the lingering memories of my adolescence took place the evening of April 4, 1968. I was at a friend's house in Richmond, Virginia, and we were making plans for the junior-senior prom, when the father of my friend came out and announced that Martin Luther King had been shot and killed in Memphis. And some cheered. One said, "That's one down. A few more to go." (He is now a district attorney in Virginia!)

Oh, I didn't join in the cheers. I had too many African-American friends on the basketball team and in classes. But I was silent. I knew that I should speak up and say something...What if it was the voice of God urging me to do so. But I didn't. I went back to the subject of making prom favors. And I went home and the what-ifs danced and partied in my head all night long. What if I would have spoken up? Would others have joined me? What if...God is calling people to live together in harmony? They danced and partied in my head all night long, and then in the morning, I heard the cock crow three times. And ever since, I have heard the "what-if's" in my ear. I still wonder what if God is still trying to get through? What if God's voice is still there, already calling unsuspecting people...like Samuel, and Simon and Andrew....and you?

What would it mean and what difference would it make? What if those "what ifs" that climb inside my ear and prance and party all night long and sing their same old What-if song...What if, in all that, is found the voice of God, the presence of God?

And what if God is not willing to give up on any one of us—on who we've been called to be, on what we've been called to do—anymore than God is willing to give up on the church?

What if God is trying to get through…even now…to you and me? What if?

When Terror Strikes

September 16, 2001

(The Sunday after 9/11)

Jeremiah 4:11-12; 22-28; I Timothy 1:12-17

11At that time it will be said to this people and to Jerusalem: A hot wind comes from me out of the bare heights in the desert toward my poor people, not to winnow or cleanse— 12a wind too strong for that. Now it is I who speak in judgment against them. 22"For my people are foolish, they do not know me; they are stupid children, they have no understanding. They are skilled in doing evil, but do not know how to do good." 23I looked on the earth, and lo, it was waste and void; and to the heavens, and they had no light. 24I looked on the mountains, and lo, they were quaking, and all the hills moved to and fro. 25I looked, and lo, there was no one at all, and all the birds of the air had fled. 26I looked, and lo, the fruitful land was a desert, and all its cities were laid in ruins before the Lord, before his fierce anger. 27For thus says the Lord: The whole land shall be a desolation; yet I will not make a full end. 28Because of this the earth shall mourn, and the heavens above grow black; for I have spoken, I have purposed; I have not relented nor will I turn back.

I Timothy 1:12-17

12 I am grateful to Christ Jesus our Lord, who has strengthened me, because he judged me faithful and appointed me to his service, 13even though I was formerly a blasphemer, a persecutor, and a man of violence. But I received mercy because I had acted ignorantly in unbelief, 14and the grace of our Lord overflowed for me with the faith and love that are in Christ Jesus. 15The saying is sure and worthy of full acceptance, that Christ Jesus came into the world to save sinners—of whom I am the foremost. 16But for that very reason I received mercy, so that in me, as the foremost, Jesus Christ might display the utmost patience, making me an example to those who would come to believe in him for eternal life. 17 To the King of the ages, immortal, invisible, the only God, be honor and glory forever and ever. Amen.

This morning's prayer was written by Bailey Wilson, a 7th grade member of our church and a student at St. Mary's Episcopal School:

Prayer:

Please help us make all of this better
Give all of us strength and help us work together
Be with all of our family and friends
And help us make this entire hatred end.
Keep everyone safe throughout all of this
And help it remain a wonderful bliss.
Please make everything get better
And help make this world come together. Amen.

E LIE WIESEL TELLS THIS STORY: WHEN THE great rabbi Israel Baal Shem-Tov saw misfortune threatening the Jews it was his custom to go into a certain part of the forest to meditate. There he would light a fire, say a special prayer, and the miracle would be accomplished and the misfortune averted.

Later, when his disciple, the celebrated Magid of Mezritch, had occasion, for the same reason, to intercede with heaven, he would go to the same place in the forest and say: "Master of the universe, listen! I do not know how to light the fire, but I am still able to say the prayer." And again, the miracle would be accomplished.

Still later, Rabbi Moshe–Leib of Sasov, in order to save his people once more, would go into the forest and say: "I do not know how to light the fire, I do not know the prayer, but I know the place and this must be sufficient."

Then it fell to Rabbi Israel of Rizhyn to overcome misfortune. Sitting in his armchair, his head in his hands, he spoke to God: "I am unable to light the fire and I do not know the prayer; I cannot even find the place in the forest. All I can do is tell the story and this must be sufficient." And it was sufficient.

This past week as been a week in which many of us also have found it difficult to light the fire; we don't know what to pray for; and we aren't even sure where a safe place is. But we do have stories. And they must be sufficient.

We have told our stories already and will tell them again and again. We will tell our children and our grandchildren. I know, for example, that my father had just walked out of a movie theater on a Sunday afternoon when he received word the Pearl Harbor had been bombed. I have heard that since I was a child. It is a family story.

What is your story? Mine began as yours did, like any other Tuesday morning. I had taken the kids to school. On the way to school I was listening to National Public Radio and there was nothing out of the ordinary. I was actually half-listening as I often do when there are children in the car. And it was only later that I realized that Aaron had heard something that I had not heard, and he asked "Daddy, what is a hijacking?" I explained to him what it was, and that was why we went through those metal detectors at airports, so that we could fly safely." I didn't think anything more of it, and I dropped them off and came in for a meeting with Virginia Dunaway, our church life administrator. We were talking about the nuts and bolts of the running of the church when Cheryl McDermott, our children's ministry director came in and said that a plane had crashed into one of the twin towers. At that point it seemed tragic, but perhaps accidental and certainly far removed, like a plane crash in California.

Fifteen minutes later she came back with the news that another plane had crashed into the other tower and suddenly the day took on a whole new meaning. A television had been set up in the presbytery office, and so from time to time I would wander by and steal a glance, but for the most part the day was a blur, hearing of another jet plowing into the pentagon. This couldn't be happening! Yet another jet downed in Pennsylvania. And then the collapse of one of the twin towers, then the other. What would be next?

We quickly decided to scrap our usual wholeness service and prepared a prayer service in case we had a few extra people. Would there be 25? 50? Let's do 100 bulletins, we said. They started arriving early, and sat here in silence. Nobody talked or visited, like we're so prone to do here in moments before worship. We just sat here broken hearted, shocked, and perhaps not even knowing why we were here. And people kept coming and coming…hundreds of men, women, and children, each with their own story that they were trying to make sense of. And it was at that service that I began to get a glimpse of a larger story. In place of all of those dreadful images that we had seen during the day, there was another image which will be indelibly etched in my mind as vividly as those others I had seen on television.

We were serving communion by intinction. Since we didn't know how many people to expect we only had one station. And as I held the bread and offered it to one after another after another I looked up and the line stretched as far as I could see…all the way to the back of the sanctuary. No music. Total silence. All waiting, yearning for something that was more than just the physical bread and juice. Call it meaning, call it something of eternal significance, call it peace, and call it love. But there you were, believers, or trying-to-be-believers in another story.

And that is why we come here today. That is why we come here on every Sunday, for that matter. It is to wrap ourselves in a story that is bigger than we are, a story that undergirds and envelops all of our personal stories, takes those stories and redeems them, placing them in the context of a powerful story that begins not on a Tuesday morning but with the words "In the beginning, God...."

And every now and then we find glimpses of our story in that larger story. Such is the case with our Old Testament lesson today. Listen to these words and ask yourself if these 2500 year old words could have been written this week:

> "My anguish, my anguish! I writhe in pain!
>   My heart is beating wildly;
> I cannot keep silent;
>   For I hear the sound of the trumpet,
>   The alarm of war.
> Disaster overtakes disaster,
>   The whole land is laid waste.
> Suddenly my tents are destroyed,
>   My curtains in a moment....
> I looked on the earth and it was waste and void;
> I looked, and lo, there was no one at all,
>   All the birds of the air had fled.
>   ...all of its cities were laid in ruins.... (Jere.4:19-26)

We aren't the first ones to live in times of turmoil, of total despair. Jeremiah was watching his world dying before his very eyes and he felt pain, he felt anger, he felt scared. A power from the east, Babylon, was looming large, disrupting life and was in the process of destroying Jerusalem, the holy city. The world as he had known it was coming to an end. It was utter chaos. Do you find something of your story in that description?

Hope did not come easily with Jeremiah; nor does it come easily for many of us. Throughout his book he argues with God, chastises God. His prayers are among the most eloquent and abrasive prayers of the Bible. And yet it is that honesty before God that enables his despair to be transformed into redemption. "The days are surely coming," he says towards the end, when all will be restored. "The days are surely coming...when...just as I watched over them to pluck up and break down, to overthrow, destroy and bring evil, so I will watch over them to build and to plant," says the Lord. (31:27-28)

Is that too good to be true? Are those just the words of a dreamy idealist? Isn't that just preacher talk? Doesn't he know the way things are in real life?

Oh, Jeremiah was grounded in reality all right. But even more deeply he was grounded in the story of a God who not only created the world but called it good; a God whose will for people was shalom, peace...wholeness...health...abundance. And that story had such a grip on him that he was able through the rubble to see an alternative vision to the despair and fear running rampant in his land and claim, in Walter Brueggemann's words, a hopeful imagination.

We can learn from Jeremiah. We must be careful not to draw too many parallels between that day and this day, for we are in uncharted territory. After Pearl Harbor we knew who our enemy was and

213

where they were; we knew what victory looked like; our shores were relatively safe; we were not under a nuclear umbrella. The times are different from Jeremiah's day, or "the greatest generation's" day, but the God is the same God.

Jeremiah's God was a large God...a robust God, a far cry from the domesticated God of our culture. And it was as Jeremiah felt the freedom to voice disappointment, forlornness, fear, and even hostility to God in prayer that the vitality of God became present and known.

God can handle our anguish. That is what so many of those passionate psalms are about, crying out to God....asking...demanding that God be God. And as they give voice to their feelings to God, they become oriented to a new reality.

That is one reason why it is important for us as people of faith to find support communities where we can feel safe to voice our feelings. It is true for our children, but it is also true for us adults as well. Our psyches have very poor digestive systems and what goes down can come up in very unhealthy ways unless they are openly and honestly addressed. That's what we began on Wednesday night here as we cancelled our regular program and shared around our tables. Many of us are finding that we are having feelings we didn't even know we had. There was one man, a veteran of World War II, who said "I thought I had forgotten how to hate; but it came back so quickly." Anger is legitimate, even called for, but if we let our anger turn to hate, then we are little better than those who have hated and hurt us. God knows it is emotionally satisfying to hate with righteous indignation, but God also knows that what is emotionally satisfying can be spiritually devastating. As Roland Bainton once said, "If you have to become the beast in order to defeat the beast, the beast has won."

We can learn well from the questions our children ask, for there is a deep honesty about them. Some of the questions I have heard as a father are: Are we safe here in Memphis? Why do bad people do things like that? Why is there evil? Did God cause that?

Let me say clearly and unequivocally, this was not God's will! God did not want those people to die. It is not part of God's plan. Jerry Falwell has been quoted as saying that this was the judgement of God coming down on America because we have been too tolerant towards minorities…too liberal…that God wanted this to happen, indeed, that God caused this to happen as he recited all of his pet prejudices….feminists, gays, doctors who perform abortion, the ACLU.

My friends, listen carefully: That is not simply a distortion of the gospel; it is a desertion of the gospel! Our God's heart was the first to break when that first airliner hit the twin tower, and it broke thousands of times over in the next few minutes.

Further, fundamentalism, be it Muslim, Jewish, or Christian is dangerous whenever the purity of dogma is placed higher than the integrity of love. No, the God of love revealed on every page of scriptures is a creative God. God does not destroy innocent lives. God may come across destruction and enter into it with us, but God is always building, always creating.

Another question children…and adults ask is about evil. Evil is real. We Presbyterians don't talk about it too much. But is it there. I don't know what it is. I don't know how to describe it. I don't know for sure what to call it. But we have seen it throughout history, and we saw it on Tuesday. On Wednesday night Bill Moyers interviewed an ethicist from a seminary and asked him "What is evil?" And the scholar replied: "Evil is when you cannot see anything of value in

215

another person." That kind of evil brought about much destruction, and our God is a creative God who will build from this, but don't let anyone tell you God is responsible for evil.

So what is to be the response of the family of faith? It is certainly prayer, but it is more than that. It is to tell the story again and again. It is the story of salvation, for this story tells of another power, even more powerful than death and evil and suffering. And it too has an image that I hope will be imprinted in your mind's eye just as those initial images of Tuesday were: it is the image of a man on a cross, and it is called "suffering love."

"This saying is sure and worthy of full acceptance: that Christ Jesus came into the world to save sinners." We hear those words just about every Sunday in our words of assurance. But is it at all possible that they have new meaning today? The salvation we are talking about here is not just the salvation from the pits of hell that some love to describe theatrically. But rather it is salvation for joy, for the full and abundant life Christ offers, knowing that God can be trusted not only with my sins and salvation, but also trusted to redeem each and every day from insignificance. God so loved the world that God sent God's son.

Let me share personally about what this means this day as I struggle to find how Christ might work for good…for salvation… in the presence of terror and evil:

Jesus saves me from judging other more harshly than I judge myself. Peace begins with me. Jesus saves me from hatred and vindictiveness toward those with whom I disagree, or who have shown hatred and vindictiveness to me. You remember the camp song of another generation: "Let there be peace on earth and let it begin with me." God can work for good, and it begins with me.

Further, Jesus saves me from indifference to the suffering of other people. As we have heard these stories of phone calls from airplanes, of firefighters giving their lives, of people wandering the streets of New York carrying pictures of loved ones, who can remain indifferent? Maybe this tragedy can put us in touch with people around the world for whom suffering is a way of life. When bombs explode in the middle east, when civil wars disrupt in Africa, maybe we can find that we are one in our suffering, and thus help God build a new world fashioned upon redemption.

Jesus saves me from a self-centered view of the world, saves me from thinking God loves me more than another. Jeremiah's God was not a tribal god, but the God of all creation. God loves the Muslims who run the sandwich shop just down the street every bit as much as God loves the Presbyterians who worship here. And it is absolutely vital that whenever anti-Muslimism or anti-Palestinian or anti-Arab bigotry raises its ugly head, we go the extra mile to expose it and confront it with suffering love.

Finally, Jesus saves me from despair, from ever believing that life has no purpose, or giving in to those impulses to abandon hope. The cross reminds us that death and despair are not dead ends, but signs of an impending resurrection, and only as we have the faith to live fully in the midst of these difficult days will be too experience resurrection and the transformation of our lives and the life of our nation. For that is our calling.

An old man in India sat down in the shade of an ancient banyan tree whose roots disappeared far away in a swamp. Soon he discerned a commotion where the root entered the water. Concentrating his attention, he saw that a scorpion had become helplessly entangled in the roots. Pulling himself to his feet, he made his way carefully along the tops of the roots to the place where the scorpion was trapped.

217

He reached down to extricate it. But each time he touched the scorpion, it lashed his hand with its tail, stinging him painfully. Finally his hand was so swollen he could no longer close his fingers, so he withdrew to the shade of the tree to wait for the swelling to go down. As he arrive at the trunk, he saw a young man standing above him on the road laughing at him. "You're a fool," said the young man, "wasting your time trying to help a scorpion that can only do you harm.

The old man replied, "Simply because it is in the nature of the scorpion to sting, should I change my nature, which is to save?"

Thanks be to God for this story that begins "In the beginning, God..." But thanks be to God, it doesn't end there. At its center there is an image of suffering love that carries us through the terror to hope and salvation. As our final hymn says:

> The soul that on Jesus hath leaned for repose,
> I will not, I will not, desert to its foes.
> That soul though all hell should endeavor to shake,
> I'll never, no never, no never forsake!

My prayer for all of you today, indeed for our whole nation, is that we will feel the loving arms of God wrapped around us, and we will know in our hearts that God will never forsake us!

Who Goes To Heaven?
Questions from the Floor

July 11, 2004

(Preached in a Summer Sermon Series on "Questions from the Floor")

John 14:1-7

"Do not let your hearts be troubled. Believe in God, believe also in me. 2In my Father's house there are many dwelling places. If it were not so, would I have told you that I go to prepare a place for you? 3And if I go and prepare a place for you, I will come again and will take you to myself, so that where I am, there you may be also.

4And you know the way to the place where I am going." 5Thomas said to him, "Lord, we do not know where you are going. How can we know the way?" 6Jesus said to him, "I am the way, and the truth, and the life. No one comes to the Father except through me. 7If you know me, you will know my Father also. From now on you do know him and have seen him."

Prayer: Holy God, in this precious hour we pause and gather to hear your word. Free us in these moments from every distraction, that we may focus to listen; that we may hear; that we may be more loving. Amen.

THE QUESTION ASKED FOR TODAY WAS submitted by several people in several different ways. Who will be saved? Do non-Christians go to heaven as we know it? Who's in and who's out? It is, of course, a little difficult to gather empirical evidence on this matter—whom are we going to interview? Do we take a poll? That's the American way! (I remember reading recently that 70% of Americans believe in angels. I guess that means angels must exist!) But Presbyterians are split on the question of who can be saved. 46% of members and 45 % of Presbyterian clergy "strongly agree" with the statement that "only followers of Jesus Christ can be saved."

Naturally, as Christians we must approach the question in a different way, starting, of course, with scripture. The word "to save" in the Greek language of the New Testament is the same word as the word for "to heal." To save is to heal. Marcus Borg therefore defined salvation as "the healing of the wounds of existence" -- the wounds we inflict upon ourselves and others; the wounds others inflict upon us; the wounds which come simply as a result of being a part of the natural world.

When most of us think of salvation, however, we think of something that happens to us when we die, but the greatest emphasis of the Bible is on salvation in and for this life on earth. The Old Testament focuses almost entirely on salvation in and for this life on earth. God has saved us, God has acted in history, our history. God has delivered us from the house of bondage into freedom. And God will continue to save us! That's salvation in the Old Testament, and for the most part, though the New Testament does address the life to come, the greatest proportion of the teaching in the New Testament continues that tradition, focusing on what we are saved from and what we are saved for in the life we are living here and now.

Wherever there is estrangement, wherever there is suffering, we are able to experience salvation that comes only from God, by God's grace.

> --If, for example, we are weighed down by guilt, salvation comes in the form of forgiveness. Several of you have told me that the high point of the worship service, the message that gets you ready for the next week, is when, after the prayer of confession, the liturgist says "In Jesus Christ, you are forgiven."

> --If, on the other hand, we are estranged from God, or from others, or from our self (which is a bitter estrangement), then salvation comes in the form of reconciliation.

> -- If we are in bondage, which can be physical, emotional, chemical (think of the power of chemical addictions- alcohol, drugs, and nicotine), or even financial bondage, salvation comes in the form of liberation from that bondage.

> --If we are victims of injustice, salvation is experienced by being made whole, being restored to the new creation that God desires for us.

All of these point to a life that can become new through God's grace; a life which is healthy, whole. A life which can then bless others. That is what God intends for all creation.

Christians, of course, believe that salvation comes through a particular act of God in history-- the birth, life, death, and resurrection, and ascension of Jesus. The fact that God would overcome the historic estrangement between God and humankind by entering fully the human condition would bring God and human together. But it was only a few decades after the death and resurrection of Jesus that salvation came to be so closely associated with dying and getting to heaven.

Why? A large part of it was the influence of the Greek philosophers upon the early church, which led to a Gnostic dualism. Everything on earth, all matter, was evil, impure. Everything "spiritual," or "other-worldly" was divine, good. It was antithetical to the Hebraic understanding of the world and the self, but it became the goal of the Christian life to simply endure this life of suffering and wait for ....salvation!

You can use a little imagination to see how this shift was made. Imagine you were born in the late first century or early in the second century....about the time the Gospel of John was written. You are very poor, perhaps even a slave. Your life expectancy might be 30 or 40 years, and it is a hard life. If you have children, there's a good chance they'll die in infancy. You work from sunup to sundown and pray you don't get sick. There are no safety nets. Your expectations of life, then, are mainly negative ones: that you can get through it without too much pain. So what is salvation to mean for them? Heaven. Heaven as consolation for the sorrows and deprivations of earth. Heaven as a good destiny that can offset the bad destiny, the fate that seems one's unavoidable lot here and now. And so through the ages, wherever there has been a life dominated by poverty and misery, the theological focus was always "pie in the sky, in the sweet by and by." And it was often those in power, such as slave owners, who emphasized this other worldly salvation so that those under them would be satisfied with their lot...

And so the question has been: How do you get to heaven? Who will be saved? Once again, throughout scriptures it becomes clear that it is God's intention that all of creation be saved, but if there is one verse that has been used to whack those not of the faith it is the one that I read earlier. "No one comes to the Father except through me.

The irony about this text is that it is set in the midst of some of the most comforting words in all of scriptures—words that are read at funerals. "Do not let your hearts be troubled. Believe in God, believe also in me." Jesus was saying good-bye to his disciples. He knew they were troubled, were wondering how they could get along without him. "In my Father's house there are many dwelling places....if I go and prepare a place for you, I will come again and will take you to myself, so that where I am, there you may be also. And you know the way to the place where I am going."

And then Thomas, bless him, said "No Lord, we don't know where you are going. How can we know the way?"

To simplify things, Jesus just said "I am the way, the truth, and the life. No one comes to the Father except through me."

It's an incredible source of comfort, as much for us as it was for them. But there are times when this text is used as a club with which we beat others over the head, or as a knife with which we can surgically sever the saved from the damned. And not just when we go after Muslims or Jews or other religions that may seem strange to us, not just outside the camp of Christianity. Sometimes we use it inside the faith as well.

223

Think of how much harm has been done by this text. How many times do you suppose people have taken that ugly strain of exclusivism in the gospel of John and just gone wild with it? A lot of evil has been done because some Christians have used it to bully and browbeat and force submission from everyone else in the world who thinks differently. The Crusades, the persecution of the Jews, the worst of some Victorian mission efforts which were often really cultural expeditions—taking woolen underwear to the Hawaiian islanders, for instance. How often have we taken those words, "the way" and interpreted them to mean "our" way, "my" way, until that way has been so narrowly and carefully staked out that you can't walk on it unless you walk sideways and single-file?

But when Presbyterians interpret scripture, we look at the text in the greater context of all of scripture, especially the greater context of the life and teachings of Jesus. And if you look at the grander context of Jesus' life, you'll find a much wider "way", a broader "way" than many of us have tended to imagine. What is "the way" he spoke of was more of an invitation than a highly-secured piece of territory? After all, Jesus did not say "This little collection of creeds about me is the way." "This little handful of propositions is the way." Not even "This religion about me is the way." He said "I am the way." I…in my complexity, I in my mystery…I in my sometimes confusing choices and priorities, I…the One forever moving toward the edges and beyond boundaries and over the top—I am the way, the truth and the life. No one comes to the Father but by this wide, broad, subversively unpredictable way. A way that is impossible to nail down and grasp a hold of, but that is forever moving like a holy wind through the lives of people and nations and races. A way that will not fit into your back pocket, (nor into a single belief system) but, if you let it, will move through you and in you until it has turned you upside down.

The Jesus that I see in the grand picture painted by the gospels is much, much bigger than the tidiest, most deliberate little interpretations of this one verse from John: "I am the way…no one comes to the Father except through me."

For I see the way of a sower who went out to sow, only he didn't place the seeds along a tidy row. He threw them every which way into the wind. Everywhere! Nothing narrow about that way.

I see the way of a man who brought children forward. There were time schedules and handlers, but he took the children onto his lap and said (more or less) "This is what my way looks like."

I see the way of a man who cavorted with all sorts of people who were on the "outs," deemed "impure" by religion, thereby broadening the way.

In short, I see Jesus, there all but on his death bed, wanting to convey that this Way is not a Way of excluding or drawing lines; it's a Way of living. And of dying.

It's funny how we have latched onto this one verse and made it the Gospel about who's in and who's out. Because there are other texts that are exclusionary, but not always to our advantage. Near the beginning of Matthew Jesus says "Not everyone who calls me 'Lord, Lord, will enter the kingdom of heaven." (Mt. 7:21) And then toward the end, his parable of the final judgment informs us that those who feed the hungry, visit the imprisoned, and clothe the naked are the ones who will sit at the throne of God's glory. (Mt. 25:31-46) It's no wonder we don't hear those made into a kind of "litmus test" for entrance into heaven. We might not fare so well!

So, where does this leave us in our initial, rather complex question of who is saved and who isn't? Let me offer just a few suggestions:

First, as we move beyond the scope of one tiny verse and see the grander scope of Holy Scripture, we see a God who is clearly for the world. Who created the world in love and saw that it was good; whose heart breaks when there is estrangement from God. We see a God whose intention is that all of creation be healed, be made whole, be saved.

Second, it is important to remember that in this text Jesus was not addressing other world religions as we know them. Oh, he would have been exposed to some Persian religions such as Zoroastrianism and Roman mythology, and some pagan religions. So to place the burden of rejection of all other faiths for all time on one saying, appearing only in John's gospel, is to place too much emphasis on one single saying.

Rather, he was addressing his followers. He was not making a general metaphysical statement about "God." He didn't say "No one comes to God except through me." He says "No one comes to the Father except through me. God here is the One whom the disciples had come to recognize in the life and death of Jesus. One scholar suggests that when Jesus says "No one..." he means "none of you." This is addressed to a particular community, not an exclusionary community. And the claim of exclusion becomes problematic when it is used to speak to questions that were never in the Gospel of John's purview.

Third, when we think of other religions, we ought to think of them with respect and take them seriously. There are sparks of the divine in many ways of knowing on earth. And who is to say that God, in God's infinite wisdom, does not work through the cultures and beliefs of other people whose view of life is very different from ours. Are all the same? Of course not. "By your fruits you shall know them," Jesus said on another occasion in Matthew. (Mt. 7:20) The truth of any religion is in the quality of life that religion brings forth from its believers and whether, from a Christian point of view, that belief bears the marks and signs of the Kingdom of God, where the whole creation exists in praise of its creator, and the people of every nation and culture do justly, love mercy, and walk humbly with God.

Fourth, we believe in a God of grace and a God of justice, and we hold those in creative tension. I have a friend who would say "Because we believe in a God of grace, we are always on the edge of universalism (that is, the belief that all are saved, no matter what). But because we believe in a God of justice, we don't quite step over that threshold."

That takes us to our final conclusion, and that is that any discussion about who is saved and who isn't, who goes to heaven and who doesn't ought to be conducted with a deep, deep humility before a God who eternally exceeds our human capacity to fully grasp. There is a mystery which cannot be explained or understood and we are better off honoring that rather than trying to fix doctrines and dogmas that wrap difficult issues like this into a neat, exclusionary package.

Some of you might remember Father Theodore Hesburgh, who was the president of Notre Dame for years. In his autobiography, he reflected on his call to the priesthood and where it had led him:

"I have traveled far and wide, far beyond the simple parish I envisioned as a young man My obligation of service has led me into diverse yet interrelated roles: college teacher, theologian, president of a great university, counselor to four popes and six presidents of the United States....I have held fourteen presidential appointments over the years, dealing with the social issues of our times, including civil rights, peaceful uses of atomic energy, campus unrest, amnesty for Vietnam offenders, Third world developments, and immigration reform.

But beneath it all, wherever I have been...I have always and everywhere considered myself essentially a priest. [Since I was first ordained in 1943] I have offered Mass every day, save one, and I have prayed the breviary each day, too. Even so, as I get older, it is increasingly clear to me that I know God all too little. I believe in God profoundly, I pray to God often, and I am grateful that God revealed God's self to us as Jesus Christ...."

"As I get older, it is increasingly clear to me that I know God all too little." Is that because he is falling away from the faith? Hardly. It is because as he grows in faith, he becomes more and more aware of the immensity of God eternally exceeding our human capacity to grasp it.

We follow Jesus because for us, He is the Way. We say that without fully understanding all that that means. It is not up to us to decide who is following the way correctly and who isn't....who will make it and who won't. We leave the faith and questions of those outside the faith to a loving, gracious God who is equal to the task.

And we dedicate our lives to following the One who comes and dwells among us, full of grace and truth, putting our energies into following the Way, sharing with others what that means to us, and working for the healing of the wounds of the world, the salvation that God so desperately desires, and that only God can ultimately provide.

Made in the USA
San Bernardino, CA
25 October 2015